ALISON'S NEW BEGINNINGS

FIONA FIELDHOUSE

otp

For my family and friends whose interest and support I have treasured over many years. And for all of us who relish a new beginning.

PROLOGUE

Alison was alone. She was very rarely alone and it was lovely. Her entire married life had been peopled by demands – her husband James' work, her children, the embassy staff, you name it. She grasped her fragile porcelain mug of Lapsang Souchong tea, scooped up a pile of estate agents' brochures and headed across the small open-plan flat to the sofa.

She glanced at her watch. James should have been home by now. It was hard to imagine James retired. He'd told her the rules years ago. On the day you reached retirement age, your employment ceased. You shed all the trappings of office – the prestige, the embassy, the chauffeur-driven car, the celebrity, the possibilities of greatness, the challenges of a demanding and effective role and sank back without trace amongst ordinary citizens.

This was to be a new beginning and Alison was used to new beginnings, only they'd never felt like her own new beginnings. They had always been James' postings, James climbing the ladder of success, James becoming more and more important. He'd initially been a First Secretary, then Counsellor, Deputy High Commissioner and finally Ambassador. Exciting in many ways, yes, but not of her choosing. It never occurred to her to expect a choice. She was happy that James had chosen her to share his life and she loved the energy there always seemed to be around him. She loved his cleverness, the way he assessed the challenges of his diplomatic role and found brilliant solutions. She loved being at his side at functions, watching as he used his urbane charm to make his case, enhance his status and ensure he made an impact on those he was meeting. She'd accepted and admired his driving ambition and had known that she and the boys would benefit from his success. Willingly and with interest and enjoyment she'd made a home wherever James was posted and opened her home to the people she was required to entertain, supported charities, learned the rudiments of new languages, organised flowers, menus, guest lists and events, come to terms with monsoons, harmattans and shamals and all the other strange and alarming weather conditions the world can present. In the early evenings she'd sit on tropical verandas loving the noise of insects in the velvet dark, the smell of jasmine, the distant downtown traffic, so far from England, but happy knowing that one day they would go home.

In the early evening she'd look at herself in a long mirror and smile, aware she was the epitome of an ambassador's wife – elegant, poised, sophisticated – but knowing that inside she was happiest being herself, a mother, a grandmother. They'd all, she and the boys, packed their boxes time and again, said goodbye to friends and dutifully followed, to foreign cities, back to London and then off again, two years here, four years there; today Kuala Lumpur next year San Francisco. The sadness of the goodbyes was a luxury she couldn't afford, so swiftly were they followed by the demands of new hellos. She focussed on her family, ensuring her sons felt secure in spite of the globe-trotting and it became second nature to her to fulfil everyone else's needs before her own. And now James had reached retirement and they'd come back to their small London flat. They were ordinary citizens.

For Alison the lack of trappings was completely balanced by having James as just James; her husband and friend, father of her children, grandfather and part of this family they had made together, with time to enjoy each other. They'd agreed they'd give themselves time to contemplate retirement before making any decisions about where they might live and what interests might involve them. And, Alison guiltily acknowledged to herself, she might actually have some choices, about where they would live, what sort of property they'd buy, who she'd make friends with. But really, she thought, slipping back into her familiar role, if James is happy, I'll be happy.

It was strange that he was so late coming back to the flat. What could he be doing? She could always call him on his mobile, but in truth she was perfectly content contemplating a new property, a new home, one she could choose herself. Contentedly she curled up on the sofa and was totally engaged with a pretty penthouse overlooking a marina when she heard James come home.

"You must look at this property," she said as he came into the room. She held up the brochure. "It could be perfect for us and just look at the view. We could have a boat. There are moorings. The boys would love that. What do you think?"

James stood, unsmiling, and said, "Ali, we need to talk."

"About what?" He hadn't greeted her, hadn't kissed her hello, took a step away from her and lowered himself into the chair opposite her. She watched him push his glasses up his nose, run his fingers through his hair, clasp his hands in front of him. She felt his tension. Carefully she put her mug on the table, her gaze not leaving her husband's face as foreboding enveloped her.

"James?"

And that's when they came, the words which fell upon her and around her like rocks from an avalanche, hurtling towards her, unstoppable, damaging, destroying, hurting the soft, trusting, loving part of her she'd given to James.

"I can find no other way to say this and no way to make it easier. I have betrayed you and for that I'm deeply sorry. I've fallen in love with someone, Ali, someone I find I can't live without."

The words seem to come from a long way off; words whose sound was not entirely coordinated with the movement of his mouth. She felt faint, felt she was falling backwards. She uncurled her legs, feet feeling for the floor and put her hands on the sofa, balancing herself, straightening her back. Bereft of speech, unable to breathe, she stared back at him. His words engulfed her as he told her of his infidelity with a young colleague, a girl of great promise he'd been mentoring and his betrayal. Her name was Elspeth. He said Elspeth now had a posting and he would be going with her. From somewhere far away in her rational self Alison thought My God, he's saying he's going to continue the globetrotting with this Elspeth strutting her stuff in her international career.

Catatonic with shock she heard him say, "You're so competent Ali, so self-contained and able and you'll be so content to be near the boys and their children and your family. Elspeth has no one. She needs me. I can give her the benefit of my experience and guide her and share the challenges." There was a roaring in her ears as she gripped the edge of the sofa. His words became meaningless until, "Beijing," he ended.

There was silence. She stared, unblinking. James got up and left the room. Alison remained motionless on the sofa, her heart racing, her breathing erratic. He came back with a shot of scotch in a glass and folded her hands round it.

"Drink this, Ali," he said. She drank. "I was planning to leave now, at once, and give you time to take this in and of course I'll take care of all the details. I promise you I won't deprive you of anything you were expecting to have when you got back to the UK."

Steadied by the whisky, she found her voice. "You were planning to leave now? This minute? You can't be serious! You really think you can say this to me, deliver this news, and away you go? Hang on a minute. James, I can't take this in. How could this happen? How long have you known her? Who is she? What did I do wrong? Not deprive me? But it's you, you…" She heard her voice break and die.

With exaggerated patience he sat down again and gave her the history of his sudden and passionate involvement with his colleague. Each word fell like a blow, spoken by her husband, her companion of thirty years who was now someone else with a voice full of determination and an urgency to be elsewhere.

"James, you can't just go. Please listen. What did I do wrong? I don't understand. Please just listen to my side."

"There are no sides, Ali. The feelings I have for Elspeth have overwhelmed me. I never expected to feel this way or to do what I'm doing. I have no choice," he finished. "There is nothing and no one that could make me change my mind."

"And the boys?" She'd cleared her throat, her voice too high as panic rose in her.

It was a while before she wept, another scotch after the closing of the door; darkness falling as the tears began; light fading as Alison felt herself fade, her being wither. This was not happening to her. This was happening to someone else. Curled up on the sofa again, property leaflets abandoned, her future snatched away, she sobbed until she was left with only the deep dry breaths of despair. The years of travelling with James, her

children's lives with their father, the future years as close grand-
parents, gentle companionship, all screwed up like a piece of
waste paper and tossed in her face. No anger. No recrimina-
tion; just information given and received. You thought your life
would be like that but no, it's going to be like this.

1

Yellow leaves, pale and lifeless symbols of the end of summer, slipped down the windscreen. The tree she'd parked beside was shedding its leaves as effortlessly as James had shed the years of their life together. Without its foliage the tree had been exposed, its true shape revealed. Without James and the trappings of his distinguished career what sort of shape would her life take? Alison took a deep breath and got out of the car. In front of her, set into a high white wall was a faded green door with a serviceable metal plate stamped 'The Stables'. Beside it was a large bell on a spring with 'Pull' painted beside the knotted rope hanging from it. She unlocked the green door and walked into The Stables. Through the small hall, she glanced into a neat kitchen on her left as she moved into the lofty space which was the ground floor. A row of casement windows ran down one side and on the opposite wall was a large fireplace with a wood-burning stove sitting under a rough oak mantelpiece.

At the end of the room, set into a soaring arch, were enormous glass doors onto a walled garden. Alison stood in the middle of the space and took a deep breath. She unbuttoned her coat and stuffed her soft tan leather gloves deep into a pocket. This is mine, she thought, turning slowly to take it all in. She felt the sense of permanence in a place which had such practical origins and thought of horses stamping hooves and swishing tails; of grooms and stable boys turning up for work on frosty mornings, opening the wide doors, clanking buckets of feed, sweeping the floor with big brooms. Bereft and uprooted, she yearned for a sense of permanence, something dependable, something which would always be there. Oh yes, she thought, I will love this place. She walked to the big arch, each footstep striking a note of intent, and thrust a key into the lock. The tall glass door swung easily on its hinges as she passed into the old yard. She saw the surface of the yard rutted with wheel lines and the serviceable walls surrounding it. The gate in the wall at the end of the yard was smothered by an elegant yellowing creeper. There was a small shed in one corner and rickety gazebo in the other. Maybe in that little corner you could catch the evening sun.

She crossed the yard to a brick-encircled roundel and ran her hand across the faded plants, pleased by their scent. Mint, how lovely, and sage. She had never grown anything, had always had a gardener when they were posted abroad and relied on silk plants in the London flat but suddenly she felt an ownership of the bedraggled herbs she was touching and was warmed by the thought that they would need nurturing. She plunged her hands in among the untidy brown stems and withered leaves, separating and noticing the difference; noticing also a snail shell and leaves which had been eaten round the edges.

Over the wall was the big house, Highvale House, now screened with trees which blotted out its view of her Stables. Above Alison was a clock tower, the clock blue in its white cupola, the hands telling the wrong time. Mmmmm. Something to be fixed. But her own clock tower. How perfectly grand! Her spirit was lifting and she felt her bruised emotions easing and sensed the embrace of the old building, her Stables, her place of refuge. But this is not just a refuge, she thought fiercely, this is the place of new beginnings. This is where I start my own adventure.

Alison wrapped her coat around her and went back into The Stables. So this is me and in spite of your energetic protestation, my sons and sisters, I've thrown off city life and I'm going to be rural. I've gone to the country for the first time in my life.

She closed the big door making sure it was locked, went up the narrow stairs and toured the first floor of her domain; a square landing and two good-sized bedrooms with a bathroom between them. She opened the window of the biggest bedroom and looked over the yard, wrinkling her nose at a pungent and unfamiliar smell. What could that be? The countryside! She leaned on the windowsill, remembering Ed's reaction to her rural intention.

"Mother," he'd said sternly, feeling the responsibility of the eldest son on his father's sudden departure from the family, "this is crazy! Stay in London. Keep the flat. You shouldn't be thinking of living alone in the country. It really is out of the question."

She'd felt his distress and wondered how much was for her and how much was for himself as he contemplated his mother as an addition to his burden of responsibility. He had a wife, two children and now a potentially dependent mother. Sadness crept up on her as she remembered him sitting in the flat where his father had sat to deliver words of betrayal and abandonment. Ed had leant forward earnestly, his dark crisp hair expertly cut, expensive suit worn easily, perfect silk tie without doubt chosen by Giselle, his high-maintenance wife. He was so like James at the same age, so ambitious, so confident, so certain of success. And Giselle was the perfect partner. Was I ever the perfect partner? Alison thought wryly.

Nick had been far less vocal but Nick, so like Alison herself, with his clear skin and deep auburn curls, was, as always, passionately immersed in his own life. He'd hugged her fiercely and said, "Mum, I will always be there for you. Anything you need, you just ask me." She'd smiled, arms round his powerful young body as she returned his hug, remembering how it had felt to hug the bonny baby, the chuckling toddler, the enthusiastic schoolboy. Darling Nick. She'd watched as he'd got into his van with 'Pentarron' emblazoned on the side and driven off into the London dusk.

With cold hands Alison closed and fastened the window, shut all the upstairs doors and made her way down the turning little staircase. Well, it was done. She'd bought The Stables and now it was up to her to get herself sorted and settle in. She locked the green door and gave a farewell tug at the bell, pleased with its joyful jangle. She stepped back to view her property in its context, discreetly set in the grounds of Highvale House. Pale sunshine lit the clock tower and shone through the small line of silver birches which stretched their branches over the wall and into the lane, their leaves continuing to drop silently on her car. She tightened the belt of her coat, turned up her collar and walked towards her car. A big, shiny black four-wheel-drive vehicle powered down the lane behind her, cascading the contents of a muddy puddle down her long camel coat as it roared by. Furious, her glow of new ownership tarnished by the muddy splash, she angrily fished a tissue from her pocket and was dabbing ineffectively at the muddy splashes when suddenly the vehicle stopped and reversed back to where she stood. Huge, immaculate and shining with chrome trimmings, the word Trailblazer streaked down its side. Well, really! What kind of trail did a person expect to blaze in rural England? She waited, watching it warily as the engine revved. A window slid open.

"Is that your car?"

"Yes."

"You're blocking the lane."

"So I am. How inconsiderate of me! And you with a trail to blaze and no doubt many more puddles to empty over unsuspecting pedestrians." The driver's arm rested on the door and fingers drummed impatiently. Alison reached her car, stopped for one final dab with her tissue, carefully opened a door and stowed her bag in the back. Taking her time, she reversed into the lane and began a slow and careful progress through the puddles, the Trailblazer impatiently close behind her. She caught one glimpse of the driver in the rear-view mirror. A man's face with an uncomfortable expression. How would you describe that face, she thought, as she swung out onto the main road and the Trailblazer roared past? Bleak, she thought. His expression was bleak. She shuddered.

AT THE AIRPORT, Alison hugged her sister and grabbed one of her bags, aware of Sally's quick appraising look.

"I'm fine, Sal, really fine, but it'll be so nice to have you for a few days. We can do lunch and shop and maybe a show…?"

"Let's get into London and your flat, Ali, before we make any plans. You know I'm not a great one for gadding and really it's you I've come to see and we should use the time getting ready for the move. I'm here to help. That's what little sisters are for: help and support and taking orders."

"Fine. We'll do that. Here's the car."

Alison smiled at her sister, pleased to have her with her, pleased to be with family, the family she'd been part of before James. Lunches and shows held no interest for Sally whose life on her husband's family flower farm in the Scilly Isles kept her happily juggling the business, her two children and family life, living in jeans and a fleece, full of energy and content with her chosen path.

Back home, Alison made coffee in the kitchen and passed Sally a mug.

"You're looking thin Ali, not that it doesn't suit you, but thin. Well, thinner. I wouldn't want you to be any more thin."

"Not slim, then? Just thin?"

"Well it's been a really hard time for you and you've got everything together so well and made your decisions, but I think it's taken its toll."

"I feel much calmer, you know. I kind of feel I know where I'm going. I mean, I know I've never lived in the country but Highvale felt sort of embracing, somehow, and I've always been good at new beginnings so I thought I might as well have another one. I do love The Stables. And it's not far from London, traffic permitting, and anyway there's always the train."

"You don't think perhaps you're running away?"

"Running away? What can you mean? It's not me who's run away, done the abandoning, run away from my responsibilities, from facing reality, from addressing the issues of retirement and ageing. Oh no. I'm not running away at all."

"So you wouldn't say you're burying yourself in the country?"

"Certainly not. And anyway, if I wanted to bury myself in the country why shouldn't I? What do you expect me to do with my life now? There's no one who needs me, who depends on me." Alison looked bleakly at her sister as she contemplated the yawning gap her words opened up. The purpose of her life was gone. No one needed her. Had that been her mistake? Had she been just so assiduous in selflessly and perfectly fulfilling James' needs that she'd perhaps emasculated him? That he'd actually felt unneeded himself? And then along came Elspeth's needs.

"You're quite sure you want to make this move?"

"I am." Somehow she would just put one foot in front of the other, take one step at a time, each day as it came.

"So when have you got the move booked?" Sally sipped her coffee

"Fortnight today."

"Great. And I presume you're doing the whole thing professionally?"

"Yes. The boys insisted. I've asked them, and Giselle of course, if there's anything they want from this flat but to be honest it's just such a sad place now they weren't really interested. Giselle quite likes that little round gilt mirror in the hall, you know the one which was on the stairs at home, and I think Ed will have some of the books. Nick is so footloose he doesn't want excess baggage of any sort so really I suppose I'll take it all with me." She looked round her sitting room, the room where her life had collapsed.

"Why don't you sell the lot and start again? Get on to a sale room and get rid of what you don't want. Have a new style. You can afford it. I will hate James forever for what he did to you, but at least he was generous with the money."

"I don't think generous is a word I could apply to James," said Alison quietly.

"I know. You're right. But what I mean is you can furnish The Stables as you like. What d'you fancy? Classic antique, oriental, minimalist or down home country?"

"Comfortable. I'd like comfortable. I don't want to show off. I just want everything to work and be what it should be; big comfy chairs that don't sag, soft rugs that don't slip, wide mirrors that bring in the light, solid tables that won't mark. And Sally, there's a herb garden in the middle of the yard. Isn't that lovely? Do you think it will bring butterflies in the summer?" A tear slid down her cheek as Sally put her arm round her shoulder.

Alison jumped up. "Enough of this. Self-pity is so exhausting, don't you think?" She turned to the sink, washing the mugs, pushing her hair off her face with the back of her hand.

"Well that's settled then," said Sally. "Let's have the estate agent's blurb about The Stables and we'll have a look at the dimensions. Could you get out your drawing pad and do some plans, do you think? You do still have a pad around, I take it? We'll make a start over a glass of wine and get a takeaway from your nice Chinese on the corner. Where's the number? I'll ring them now."

ALISON WAS amazed it all happened so quickly. She was keeping her small decorative pieces, her glass and china, and everything else was destined for sale rooms and house clearance. The new chairs, tables, mirrors, beds and bed linen were chosen, ordered and ready for delivery on moving day. Today. Nick was here and she was ready to go.

"OK, Mum? Got your mobile, got your keys? Let's go." Nick held open the door and she left the flat without a backward glance, determined footsteps on the stairs, out into early-morning London. She squeezed into the passenger seat of her packed car, quietly closing the door with a feeling of finality tinged with déjà vu. It used to be Alison driving a car packed with the boys' stuff and heading for school or university or otherwise facilitating a change in accommodation.

"Ahead of the rush hour and going in the right direction against the traffic," said Nick with satisfaction, driving expertly out of the square and into the main flow of cars and buses. He loved it when things went according to plan. "So here we go, Mum. New places are good stuff, don't you think? I think you're doing the right thing and don't understand why Phillips and Ed have been so set against it."

"They've been talking to you then, have they?"

"Yeah. I said to Ed, come on, you have as much influence with Mum as I do. You say what you want to her and I'll say what I want. But your sister! She's something else. She's so unlike Sal. Phillipa doesn't think you'll cope with the country. I mean, really! All those years abroad with Dad, finding your way about new places, getting us settled, making new friends. This will be a doddle. This is England, after all."

"I suppose I feel grateful that people care enough about me to worry, Nick, and being the eldest Phillipa has always told me and Sally what we should be doing. She's a great organiser, your aunt but, and here comes one of my platitudes, her heart's in the right place."

"Shoulder to the wheel, hey Mum, and nose to the grindstone."

"Exactly. And a bit of not counting your chickens until they're hatched or crossing that bridge until you've come to it. I think Phillipa's worry has been the country thing. All the places we lived in overseas were in cities, remember? We were urban expats, weren't we? City life anywhere these days has similarities. Phillipa thinks I'm not going to manage with rural England and secretly, Nick, subliminally if you like, she's losing a lovely London opportunity with me moving out. She's found using the flat very useful! After all, everyone has their own agenda in life." Alison settled back in the car as the light increased and eased her feet round the bags on the floor. "But your brother's a darling and feels very protective and I'm grateful."

"So what's his agenda in life?"

"He's got a lot on – wife, children, mortgage, career. I certainly don't want him to feel I'm adding to his burden and I've said I'll go down and mind the children any time."

"So why *did* you pick the country, Mum?"

"To be honest I didn't pick the country and it doesn't seem any different from anywhere else to me. I picked The Stables and something different, something new. I've always enjoyed a challenge. Highvale isn't really the country, is it? I can get the newspaper delivered for goodness' sake." She instantly regretted her irritable tone.

There was silence between them as Nick slid the car onto the motorway and eased over into the fast lane. She watched him as he drove, his hair shorn of any hint of the curls he'd had as a child, curls so like her own.

"I loved London, you know, when I was young. Going to live in London was my dream and that was why I jumped at the chance to live here when my uncle introduced me to his company and I learned to draw maps. What about your agenda in life, Nick, your hopes and dreams?"

"If I can make a living doing something I love, that's good enough for me. I don't see the point of spending whatever time I have on the planet working my arse off to buy stuff. I think you've got to have a passion, be really involved. And right now this veteran car business is what I love. And I'm good at it, Mum. It takes me all over the place; I meet great people and I'm not stuck within four walls."

"But isn't this just a rich man's pastime? You seem to me to be very reliant on one rich man and vulnerable to any whim of his."

Nick glanced in the wing mirror, pulled into the outside lane to pass a slow truck and then back into the middle lane again. "I don't blame you for thinking that. But Charlie Pentarron's a great guy. He's made his money in the pop industry and doesn't need to do that anymore and he really feels he can use his fame as well as his fortune to do great things; doesn't want publicity for himself, but wants to raise money for good causes. And what's wrong with doing that and enjoying life at the same time? He's got this company which is into big events and rallies and races and merchandising and a huge amount of stuff all linked to veteran and vintage cars. And I was in on this at the start. I've got what he needs. My engineering degree was my 'in', but now I'm going to do some business and management qualifications too. This whole business is growing."

Alison was warmed by his enthusiasm and his confidence. "Good for you. It sounds great."

"It is great. I'm going on the next Beijing to Paris rally and I'll be sorting out all the logistics as well as being involved with the mechanical back-up and the publicity. It's been going every three years since Renault put out a challenge in 1907. You have to pay almost fifty grand to enter. Not a problem for Charlie, of course, but he'll raise more than that. And you should see these cars, Mum. They're really cool; amazing veteran cars, built by hand before 1904 and still going like they were made yesterday. And the Edwardian ones, built before 1918. And the vintage class, built up to 1930. The guys really have to know their stuff to be sure the whole car is genuine, all the parts and everything. Cars are bought and sold for huge sums. I just love the flexibility of the work; the travel, the people, everything. Charlie's given me a really fair contract, and I'm happy with that."

Nick's positive vibes warmed her as they headed west.

"Here's the sign for Highvale." They negotiated their way round the village and Nick stopped the car down the lane from The Stables.

"Great. The removal company's here already." He banged on the driver's window. "Hi there! Good to see you. D'you want to come in?"

Alison waited, key in hand, until they all gathered outside her door.

"Just a minute." She put her hand on the bell rope, paused and then ceremoniously gave the rope a hefty pull. "Hear that? A truly joyful jangle. Let's go in."

The day was a long one full of effort but Alison had done this many times and with the muscle of Nick and the removal men at her disposal the place was soon manageable. By the time the removal men left, main pieces of furniture were positioned, cardboard containers in the right rooms ready for unpacking and a bed for her and one for Nick were ready to sleep in.

"Time to hit the pub!" she said to Nick.

A CRACKLING fire spitting onto a wide-flagged hearth gave heartening warmth and the movement and noise of people in the small bar was reviving as Nick and Alison ate the landlord's recommended fish and chips.

"Not bad," said Nick.

"I was so hungry, anything would taste heavenly." Alison raised her glass. "Thank you darling for all your help. Couldn't have managed without you and tomorrow you can be off without a care in the world." She shivered. "Where's that draught coming from? Is there a door open?" She looked over her shoulder and saw a group of people come through the open door, the last one closing it. Led by a tall man shrugging himself out of an ancient waxed jacket which he dumped on a chair, his companions, a group of women of a certain age, clustered round him at the bar or found seats nearby.

"A bottle of your house red, if you please John, and..." he turned to those nearest him, "any apple juices or coffees or anything?"

Alison watched as, like sparrows, they fluttered and settled and the tall man held court from a bar stool. She could see well-worn cowboy boots under his faded jeans, a sagging sweater with a purple polo neck emerging from it and long-fingered hands warming the wine in his glass. His hair was long, grey streaks frosting its dark richness. His face, in spite of his light friendliness, looked strained, deep grooves casting shadows from his nose to his smiling mouth. One of the ladies, tall and elegant, with short hair and long beaded earrings, stood and held up her glass.

"To Aidan. It's lovely to get together again and thank you for all the planning you've put into this term. We've all been looking forward to your bricks-and-mortar course and today has been a really good start." A murmur of agreement and a sipping of drinks followed. The tall man graciously inclined his head, raised his glass in return and smiled.

"Well, it'll be demanding, to be sure. Buildings are hard to draw and paint but I want you all to get the very best out of it and out of yourselves. And who knows, maybe we'll have enough to put something together for the Christmas Fair."

"Shall we go, Mum?"

Alison obediently pushed back her chair and stood, tall and elegant in her knitted russet cardigan and dark narrow trousers, her fine gold bangles giving a tiny tinkle as she returned the chair to its place and pulled on the soft woollen jacket that had been hanging from it.

"I'll go and pay at the bar." She watched Nick as he went to the bar and again noticed the tall loose-limbed man on his high stool and as she mused over who he was and why he was there, she saw he was looking directly at her – smiling, amused. Flushing, she looked away, studied the polished brass objects on the wall and then moved towards the fire, holding out her hands in front of it and rubbing them gently together. In the mirror above the fireplace, she saw him lifting his glass to her. He raised an eyebrow and took a sip from the glass and, amused by his sardonic air and his battered cowboy boots, she smiled too. Life is to be lived, she thought. But where's Nick? I'll be doing no living at all if I don't get some sleep. The sparrows were fluttering and taking their leave, picking up bags, conversing in twos or threes, checking watches, buttoning jackets, zipping zips. Going home, thought Alison. To where? To whom?

ALISON OPENED THE WINDOW, turned off the light and lay in her bed listening to the new and unfamiliar noises of a country night. She heard the wind in the trees, the fading murmur of a vehicle in the distance, a gathering silence in the deep darkness. All the complexity of her life, the hopes and disappointments, joys and sadnesses, the clutter of the human condition, stilled, as the silence continued. Drained of energy, drained of emotion, she felt her body sink into sleep, her mind empty, her future unoccupied but waiting.

2

Alison had become familiar with waking before dawn in the first weeks at The Stables. This morning she could hear a bird singing in the darkness; surely not a nightingale? Maybe the birdsong meant it was nearly daylight. She rolled over and drew the cover about her, the loneliness of her bed gnawing at the edges of her initial sense of peace. She was feeling her way into her new routine and determinedly not looking backwards, determinedly refusing to acknowledge her anger. At times she felt unreal, the ground shifting a little beneath her feet, hearing her own voice coming from somewhere behind her, but focus on practical things helped. The minutiae of domesticity soothed and brought stability.

The light grew, illuminating her bedroom, shades of cream and ivory with painted furniture and a large mirror with a plain pale frame over a wide chest of drawers. Two double cupboards down one side of the room were panelled with creamy textured fabric, matching the curtains which were simply pinch pleated and piped in pale pistachio. On the wall hung white fretwork shelving, with her Augarten porcelain, shiny white and edged with green, each piece bearing a small pink rosebud. She couldn't bear to part with it but it was too pretty and delicate for the big space downstairs. In one corner sat her low button-back chair, now upholstered in a green and cream check with the occasional tiny pink flower. The wood-work in the room was white and shiny and she could see the shape of the round porcelain handle on the door emerging from shadow.

As the light increased, she heard something above her. What was it? There it was again. She sat up. Rustling and scuf-fling. She lay back quietly as the noise tracked back and forth round one side of the ceiling. There was definitely something up there. The attic space had looked fine when she and Nick stored the last of the boxes. What a bore. Something else to get sorted out. It might be rats. Maybe there were rats which had lived here for generations, lived on the horses' feed. It could be a real problem. She already had a clock expert coming to start up the clock in the tower and clearly needed some sort of gardener and now a rat assassin was required. Next stage of rural idyll coming up. It wasn't like this in India. Oh no. In those good old days, the 'memsahib' days, the Mr Fix-It, the Misteri, was summoned and took care of everything. Oh well. Don't let the grass grow under your feet.

As the first platitude of the day arrived she smiled, threw back the cover, slid her feet into the slippers by her bed and shrugged on a warm dressing gown, pulling the belt tightly about her. Light rhythmic slap of slippers on stairs, comfort-able shuffling of slippers over flagstones and tiles, click of a switch, somnolent hiss of the kettle as it started up, sigh of the fridge door when she closed it, clink of her mug, her lovely thin porcelain mug covered with pale overblown roses now waiting beside the kettle and then the loveliness of hot tea. A symphony in grey and white, she thought, that's what this kitchen is, and it pleased her to see plain white cupboard doors, uncluttered shiny grey granite surfaces, an elegant little orchid in the corner and warm touches of red in the tea towel, the round red frame of the mirror which echoed the window, the bowl of plums and the naïve print of the four seasons of an apple tree on the wall above the cooker. She was pleased she'd left the window uncovered. Almost impossible to curtain a round window successfully anyway, but waiting for the kettle to boil she could see the birds flying in and out of the bird feeder outside the window. A flurry of blue tits were suddenly dispersed by a nuthatch which energetically used its sharp beak to make the most of its time on the swinging structure and then, in a flash, peanut in beak, it was gone and the blue tits companionably fluttered in again.

Alison took her tea into the sitting room, occupied now by a simple wooden dining table and chairs and a large dresser at the kitchen end of the room. Two big sofas and a couple of bulky easy chairs occupied most of the rest of the space and some pretty armchairs upholstered in an outsize peony print added zing. She put her mug on the coffee table, zapped on the television and pulled the curtains back from the windows. Nice morning, but what a mess that yard is. Must get a gardener. Hey ho, better make a list.

Watching TV and sipping her tea, hot, thin refreshing liquid, in her delicate mug, she thought how much nicer tea tastes if you slurp it. She held the mug in both hands and slurped again. That's what life should be like really, sucked in noisily in joyful gulps. But her resolve to feel contentment in small things began slip and an all-too familiar heaviness settled on her. No, no. Come on. Banish those thoughts of James and memories of the comfort of togetherness. No point. She blew her nose. Start the list.

Scenes of famine, deprivation and aggression were flashing at her from the TV and in the face of a bewildered tearful child she switched it off. I can't take it, she thought. The world is such an awful place. Will that child ever know joy or will its short experience of life be overwhelmed with hunger, thirst and fear? Quiet contentment with the small things in life began to seriously evaporate and she knew action was the only way to stop the downward slide of her mood. Time to get on with the day.

The clock expert came at 10.00. His name was Bill Dixie. He was a large, thick-set man with white hair and dark bushy eyebrows which moved independently as his face echoed his speech.

"Good morning Mrs Henderson," bushy eyebrows disappeared up into hairline as he smiled, bowed slightly from the waist, straightened. One eyebrow descended, "and how are we today? Nice morning for it," both eyebrows settled, awaiting her response.

"Hello Mr Dixie. Do come in." She held the door wide and he looked doubtfully at the pale floor and then down at his working boots. One eyebrow jiggled.

"I'm not so sure you'll thank me for coming through here with these boots, let alone my kit and my ladder. Is there any way I can get round the back?"

"I do have access through a gate at the back. You're right. That might be easier than dragging your ladder all the way through here. Perhaps you could drive your van down the lane there and a short way up the drive? You'll see my gate and I'll meet you out at the back."

Alison switched on the kettle as she passed the kitchen and zipped up her quilted body-warmer. In the yard, she unlocked the garden door and heard Mr Dixie's truck rattle to a stop. The ladder clanked and slid as he shuffled it sideways through the gate and stood it against the wall and then joined Alison in the yard to look up at the clock.

"That's a handsome clock, Mrs Henderson."

"It is, isn't it? I really love it. I love its blue face and the white cupola and the little leaded dome with the weather vane on top. Would you be able to check that the weather vane is moving easily while you're up there?"

The eyebrows met over Mr Dixie's nose and parted again. "Well, I can tell you if it's moving or stuck but I wouldn't necessarily be able to fix it, clocks being my business you know, not weathervanes."

"Understood." She smiled. "Tea or coffee Mr Dixie?"

"Tea and two sugars would go down a treat Mrs Henderson. Thank you very much. Now, what I'm going to do is get up there and have a shufti and then I'll come down and tell you what I think. OK?"

"That'll be fine. Thank you."

"I can't tell you how long it'll take me or when I'll be back to do it, mind."

"That's OK. Just open this door and call me when you need me."

ALISON WAS WORKING her way through *The Parish News* and *The Highvale Herald* looking for advertisements for gardeners when she heard two voices in the yard. Strange. Who could that be? Outside, there was a man standing in the gateway calling up to Mr Dixie.

"I say, is this your truck?"

"Hello there," Alison moved into the yard. The man remained in the gateway. Alison took in the country jacket, flat tweed cap, mustard coloured cord trousers. He took the cap off his iron grey hair and gestured with it. Alison smelt exhaust fumes and could hear a heavy engine and barking dogs on the other side of the wall.

"This truck here. Do you realise it's parked on private property? This is the rear driveway to my house and this truck is blocking my way."

"No," said Alison. She could hear Mr Dixie coming down his ladder.

"No? What do you mean, no?" barked the man with mustard trousers.

"I mean I don't know the truck is on private property and I didn't know it was blocking your way." She walked towards him with her hand outstretched. "I'm Alison Henderson."

"Oh, are you? I am the owner of this land and your truck has no right to be here." He remained in the gateway, his hands on his hips. Alison put her hands in her pockets. Mr Dixie joined her.

"Well now. The truck is mine, sir, and it's there because I had to get my ladder in to get on to Mrs Henderson's roof. As she says, we had no idea this was private land. May I ask who you are, sir?"

"I am Air Vice-Marshal Rowbottom." Hands by his sides and chin up, he said, "I own Highvale House and this lane is my lower driveway and I would be obliged if you would remove this truck forthwith."

Alison looked at Mr Dixie. His eyebrows were completely level and very still.

"I will move my truck to permit you to pass through sir, and I will be advising Mrs Henderson, who has only recently moved into The Stables, to get her deeds checked. It would surprise me if she has no right of way across this land."

"I couldn't give a damn how surprised you are. Just get your truck out of my way."

Mr Dixie's eyebrows began to meet over his nose, but he dug his keys out of his pocket.

Air Vice-Marshal Rowbottom disappeared and the noise of the powerful engine and barking of dogs grew louder. What an unpleasant man. She went through the house and opened the front door for Mr Dixie.

"Well, what a nice welcome that was Mrs Henderson. Very neighbourly, I must say."

"I'm sorry, Mr Dixie. I had no idea about this."

"Well if I were you, m'dear, I'd get on to the solicitor and just check those deeds. I would expect you to have a right of way since there's a gate there that's been there for a long time. And don't you worry, I shall be taking my ladder out the way it came in."

A brief jiggle of the eyebrows and he was back up his ladder. By the time he came down with his assessment, Alison had found a vermin control company and booked three gardeners to come to give estimates. The unpleasant Air Vice-Marshal was far from her mind.

"Well Mrs Henderson, I've had a good look at your clock. It's quite a small space up there and the mechanism is a little bit apart from the clock face. I've checked out the transmission rods and wires and it'll all need a good clean and oil but it's nothing too serious. So there you go, Mrs Henderson. I can get the small part that's needed and we'll have your clock going in no time. Now, would you like to hear your chimes, just the once, before I go?" His smile was wide, eyebrows way up his forehead and his eyes gleamed with pleasure.

"Oh that would be lovely, Mr Dixie. Yes please." Alison stood in the yard and watched him go up the ladder and onto the roof. Then, entranced, she listened to the chimes, clear simple sounds beating out the hour. I love it, she thought. My clock has a voice. I have a joyful bell at my front door and these friendly chimes on my roof.

Suddenly the clarity of the simple chimes was jarred by discordant hooting. Several short furious blasts interrupted the chimes. Alison turned and looked through the open back gateway. A large black vehicle was nudging Mr Dixie's truck. It was the Trailblazer which she had encountered in the lane the day she took ownership of The Stables.

"Mr Dixie," she waved to him on the roof, and shouted through cupped hands. "It's the truck problem again I'm afraid." She walked to the gate. The window of the black vehicle slid open.

Alison looked into the clear grey eyes of the man behind the wheel, the man with the bleak expression. Hmm, she thought. A man of the chiselled features variety. Crisp hair impeccably brushed; level eyebrows; a straight mouth, no hint of a smile.

"I take it you're the new occupant of The Stables," he said, his words dropping from the height of his vehicle. A rude, impatient person. Alison was irritated and she allowed her irritation to fuel her reply.

"I don't actually see myself as an occupant," she said pleasantly, "I am the new owner, the new resident." She folded her arms, her head inclined to one side, meditating. "No, I am not occupying this property but I live in it. This is my home and it is my intention," she paused and drew a deep breath, "to dwell here." Good word, she thought. "Dwell," she repeated. Not passing through, but dwelling, in a permanent sense. "Now if you would kindly reverse your tank of a vehicle," she waved dismissively at the four-by-four, "for a brief moment, Mr Dixie here will just pop his ladder onto his truck and be off and you can scuttle up this lane or lower driveway or whatever you call it and blaze your trail unimpeded."

She turned her back on him and began a warm and grateful farewell to Mr Dixie.

"Thank you so much, Mr Dixie. Do you think you have everything, all your tools and oh look, here's your jacket. No, no, I'll bring it to your truck."

The Trailblazer reversed down the drive and hovered in the lane, engine running and driver watching Alison. Even from this distance she was aware of his impatience and sensed his tension. The man's entire energy seemed taken up with his brusque intolerant attitude. He seemed consumed with restlessness. Well, other people had priorities too. Alison courteously saw Mr Dixie's equipment into his truck. She tested the back of the truck like an expert, fingering the bolts and shaking the chains to make sure the tail flap was secure and then, once he was aboard, talking to him through his window and reconfirming their arrangements. In the wing mirror of the truck, she could see the driver of the four-by-four fuming as he revved his engine and grasped his steering wheel, ready to turn back into the drive. At last, Alison released Mr Dixie who reversed slowly and carefully down the drive and she waved prettily as he passed the Trailblazer and then she swiftly whisked into her yard and closed the gate in the wall, smiling as she heard the Trailblazer grind its way up the drive.

It was a small triumph, but Alison felt her stress levels rising. She'd never encountered neighbourly confrontation before. What a nightmare to have to constantly come into contact with someone who was so unpleasant to you. And what a nuisance to have to keep informing someone of your deliveries. Sharing access to the back of her property was becoming annoying and very unsettling. Also unsettling was sharing her home with its unseen occupants and hearing the pattering of tiny feet in the ceiling, which happened eerily at the same time before dawn every morning.

THE DAY of reckoning for the rats dawned. The stable clock was striking as the doorbell jangled. Alison opened the door.

"Oh." Her voice fell. "Hello. I thought you were the rat assassin from vermin control."

A sweet-faced plump young woman in overalls smiled at her in a bewildered fashion. "Hello," she said, "I am. I'm from Green Planet Pest Control. I'm Charlotte."

"Oh. You aren't at all what I imagined."

"Well, we abandoned the balaclavas and Kalashnikovs a while back." Charlotte grinned. "Now it's overalls and plastic gloves."

Alison laughed. "I'm so pleased you're here. Come in."

Charlotte toured the building, crept about in the attic space, flashed her torch into nooks and crannies and expertly placed her bait. Before she left she made an appointment for the next visit.

"Do you feed the birds, Mrs Henderson?"

"Oh yes. I have a feeder outside my kitchen window. I love seeing them swoop in and out."

"Best sweep up under the feeder about tea time every day. Bird feeders attract rats. Only put out a small amount each day and be careful what you put on the compost heap."

"Oh, I don't think I have one of those."

"You don't? But you have a garden. What do you do with your tea bags and potato peelings? They should be going on your compost."

Alison was suitably chastened. "Charlotte, you must without a doubt be the most charming rat assassin in the business and I'll certainly look into having a compost heap."

Charlotte drew a small card from the pocket of her overalls. "Here's my card. This lists our other services too." Alison accepted the card. C. Smith.

"Interesting," she said. "I'm intrigued, Charlotte. How on earth did you get into pest extermination? And is the C for Charlotte?"

"Certainly is. But I do this with Charlie. It's a bit of a long story, but I was number crunching in the City and one day this bastard ran into me on my bike. Didn't stop. Luckily someone dialled 999 fast and I'm OK. But I did a lot of thinking and lots of things changed in my head. So I changed my life. Did a post-grad environmental course, came out here, met Charlie and now we've started a business. We both do everything from the hands on to the marketing and finance."

"That is really impressive."

"Glad you think so. Don't forget the waste recycling! Look forward to seeing your compost heap next time."

Charlotte left and Alison added compost to the growing 'To Do' list.

THE GARDENERS who answered Alison's invitation to talk about her garden were less of a surprise. The first was a man with a rackety old truck with Highvale Landscapes emblazoned on its door, a silent boy following glumly in his wake. Then there was a shifty looking individual with a woollen cap down to his eyebrows, multiple facial piercings and a strangely scented squashed looking cigarette adhering permanently to his lower lip even when he spoke. Lastly there was a taciturn but willing young man who would have tugged his forelock if he'd had one. As a total novice, Alison was hard pushed to make a proper assessment of each of them and make her choice. The Highvale Landscapes truck driver alienated her by calling her 'love' with a metaphorical pat on the head and announcing condescendingly that he'd have her sorted in no time. The forelock tugger seemed to know less than she did and failed totally to inspire her confidence. To her surprise, she warmed to Jake in the woollen hat in spite of his shifty appearance because of the way he paused and considered carefully before he said a word. She liked the way he walked round her small garden as if he were communing with the plants rather than with her and he seemed less interested in saying what he thought she might like to hear and more interested in giving her his candid opinion and sharing his knowledge. This done, he gave her an articulate outline of what he'd do with the garden, were it his, and she liked his ideas.

"How do you know so much about gardening?" asked Alison.

Jake carefully squeezed the cigarette stub between finger and thumb and put in his pocket. "Well, last year I finished an RHS course. You know the RHS?" She shook her head. "Royal Horticultural Society. I did the RHS Advanced Certificate in Horticulture and included Planning Layout and Construction of Ornamental Gardens as one of my modules. You have such a perfect space here, neglected but with great potential. I'd love to give you a hand with it."

"I'll let you know." She was intrigued. What was he? An ex-con who'd done a Government-assisted course? A rock musician who'd fallen on hard times? Or simply someone who was changing the direction of his life, just as she was. Oh yes. He had to be the one. After the pretty rat assassin, it was entirely appropriate that the gardener was unconventional too.

"Oh Jake," she said before he left, "do you know about compost? I'm told I should have a compost heap and to be careful of rats."

He smiled. "You have to get the soil right first off and good compost is gold dust."

Alison went to the list by the phone and crossed off 'Find gardener'. Only one item remained. 'Check out right of way behind The Stables.' There was no way round it. She was going to have to confront the mustard-trousered Air Vice-Marshal.

3

The clock had been working for less than twenty-four hours when a furious complaint sliced into Alison's early-morning routine. Air Vice-Marshal Rowbottom's steely voice rasped from the telephone.

"May I ask why you have your clock striking the hour through the night? Do you not realise what an intrusion this is to your neighbours? You've kept the whole damn village awake."

"I am so sorry. I had no idea the chime would be so loud during the night. I've had a disturbed night too, and I'll get on to Mr Dixie at once and have the problem rectified."

"And you can tell him not to park his pestilential truck on my lower drive while he's about it." The phone went dead. Alison was irritated. She fully acknowledged her mistake but really, it wasn't necessary to be quite so rude. Fortunately, Mr Dixie could come at once and even more fortunately a letter from the solicitor arrived that morning confirming that she did have right of way and the right to park for the purposes of property maintenance.

Alison decided a visit to Highvale House was indicated, for

a personal apology but also to show the Air Vice-Marshal the
letter from the solicitor. As soon as Mr Dixie had adjusted the
clock, reloaded his ladders and driven off in his pestilential
truck, she set off up the front drive. She certainly would not
approach from the lower one.

It was pleasant walking up the road and Alison tasted the
fresh clean air and enjoyed a sense of freedom and a contented
feeling that she was in the right place. She liked the sound of
her boots rhythmically striking the surface of the road and the
feel of the cold air on her cheeks as she swung her arms and
strode purposefully alongside a laid native hedgerow, amused at
the surprise of a small rabbit and the beady eyes of a robin
watching as she passed. The difficult minutiae of settling in
were being sorted out and she was less often aware of her
anger and her bruised emotions.

She turned into a sweeping drive and walking under vast
old lime trees, reached Highvale House and pulled a big brass
knob to ring the doorbell. She stood on the top step, confident
and poised and determined to be civilized and charming and
not let a neighbourly dispute spoil a good start to her new life.
There was a warm smile on her flushed face as she prepared to
speak. The bell was answered by manic dog barking and
through the stained glass of the front door she could see the
frenzied jumping of Labradors. A piping voice issued
commands which, when the voice reached a pitch of hysteria,
were finally obeyed. The door was opened by a small figure,
arms straining to hold the dogs. Alison could smell baking and
old-fashioned floor polish.

"Hello. I'm Alison Henderson. I live at The Stables and I
wondered if it was possible to see Air Vice-Marshal
Rowbottom."

"Come in, come in. Don't mind the dogs, but I can't let
them out when the gate's open." She closed the door, released
the dogs, pointed down the hall and with her voice at its hyster-

ical pitch commanded, "In your beds." They went. Alison took off her gloves and held out her hand.

"Hello," she said again, "I'm Alison."

The small thin woman, straight fair hair simply cut with a side parting, wore a blue sweater, its polo neck large on her bony shoulders, a tweed skirt which hung loosely, thick country stockings and sensible soft-soled shoes which squeaked quietly on the polished tile floor. She, too, held out her hand. "Virginia Rowbottom. Welcome to Highvale. My husband's out but I'm expecting him back shortly. Won't you have a cup of tea? Come into the kitchen. It's warmer there."

The kitchen was large and square with a table covered with flowered oilcloth and piled with cake tins and cooling racks. Warmth came from an Aga festooned with tea towels and oven gloves, a mantel shelf above it with pretty old plates, candlesticks, a vase of bright berries and an assortment of postcards, invitations and memos chaotically tucked behind everything. There were dogs' beds near the back door, flower-pots on the window sills, and on a large dresser an impressive row of screw-top glass storage jars containing everything from tea and coffee to innumerable types of pulses and pickles. Above a big white Belfast sink was a loaded plate rack and on the draining board were upturned saucepans, wooden spoons, baking trays and glass mixing bowls. Virginia lifted a lid of the Aga and pushed the kettle on to a hotplate, indicating a chair for Alison.

"Just dump your coat over there. Now, how are you getting on? I'm sorry I haven't been over to see you. We have two daughters, Melissa and Annabel, and I've been here there and everywhere getting them sorted one way and another."

They exchanged information about their families, pleas-antly interested in one another, but Alison volunteered no information about James and was grateful that Virginia asked no questions. Alison, fortified by the Earl Grey tea she was sipping from a wide porcelain cup, asked about Air Vice-Marshal Rowbottom.

"Has your husband mentioned the little difficulty we had?"

"There are always difficulties with my husband. He is a very organised man and accustomed to command and now he's retired I think he sees Highvale as his command. When he retired I stood in this kitchen and clearly said to him that this is my domain and here I am in command." Virginia smiled wearily. "Tell me about it."

Alison told her, explained that the clock had been adjusted and showed the letter.

"Tell Robert all that when he comes in and let's hope everything will be OK. Now, are you settled into The Stables nicely and what will you be doing now you're here?"

"Well I hadn't thought that far ahead, really. The house is pretty well sorted and I'm looking forward to learning about the garden. I've spent the last thirty something years abroad, postings here and there, and I suppose now's the time to look for new interests."

"So you've been a trailing spouse too, have you? This is the first house I've lived in that I've actually been able to choose things for and what a joy it is to know that some faceless commander on high is not going to get it into his head that Robert should be given a new posting." There was perfect understanding between them. "Now there's lots to do here in Highvale. The church is very active, the Women's Institute, the Garden Club and of course there's Aidan's art classes."

"Aidan?"

"Yes. Aidan Forester. He's become a professional painter and runs courses to supplement his income. Lives just past the shop on the Green. His wife still lives in London, very high-powered woman, God knows what she does, but she's hardly ever here. The daughter visits and sometimes the son, but Aidan just drifts about really, doing his painting, organising exhibitions when he's got the motivation, and running his courses, which people seem to love."

"I think I may have come across him with his class in The Huntsman one evening. Is he a tall, rather unconventional looking man?"

"Absolutely. Jeans and cowboy boots, usually. Drives about in a clapped-out old BMW. Calls it the Beamer."

Both looked up as they heard a car drive up. The dogs leapt out of their beds and raced for the door.

"Robert." Virginia's mouth was a thin line. "Best to talk to him in here." She put the kettle on the hotplate again. The entry of Robert Rowbottom was turbulent. Alison heard the front door open and slam shut; heard the booming voice uttering dog speak and the heavy footsteps on the tiled floor heading towards the kitchen.

"Virginia?"

"In here." Man and dogs erupted into the kitchen. He strode to the back door and the dogs ecstatically ran out.

"Gate's shut," he said to Virginia.

"Hello Robert. Alison's come to see you."

"Alison?" He turned to look at the visitor. Alison smiled and stood, holding out her hand.

"Alison Henderson. From The Stables."

"Ah yes. The infernal clock chiming and the pestilential truck."

Alison continued to hold out her hand and looked calmly at him. His wife sipped her tea and watched.

"Robert Rowbottom." He took her hand in a firm grip and shook it, then looked at his wife. "Any tea going?"

"Sit down Robert and listen to Alison." She poured his tea as he scraped a chair up to the table and leaned back on it. Alison returned to her chair.

"I would like to apologise for the disturbance the chiming of my clock caused you." She smiled at Robert Rowbottom. "I was so pleased that Mr Dixie was able to get it going so easily. It's such a lovely ornamental thing but the history of The Stables, its essence if you like, is that of a practical working environment and it seemed right that the clock should be working again. On the day that Mr Dixie was mending it there was some unexpected conflict to do with his truck and I'm afraid it put him off his stride a little. He said to me when he came back this morning to make the adjustment that he would usually, as a matter of course, ask the client if a clock such as this should have the chimes overridden during the night hours. He's adjusted my clock so that now it will stop chiming at ten and start again at nine in the morning. Will that be acceptable to you, Mr Rowbottom?"

Robert Rowbottom looked at his wife who looked impassively back at him. He shifted in his chair, ran his fingers through his wiry grey hair, squared his shoulders and cleared his throat.

"That sounds in order." He picked up his teacup.

"Thank you," prompted Virginia, looking at her husband, who studiously drank his tea. Alison smoothed out the solicitor's letter in front of her. Robert Rowbottom looked at her warily.

"Any cake?" he asked his wife.

"Alison, would you like to try my fruitcake?" Virginia pulled a tin towards her and fetched some plates.

"Thank you. Baking has such a lovely homely smell, doesn't it?" She smoothed the letter again.

"Well?" barked Robert Rowbottom testily. "You've clearly got something else to say."

Alison slid the letter across the oilcloth towards him and let it speak for itself. He read in silence and pushed it back to her.

"Mrs Henderson…"

"Alison, please," she interrupted, smiling.

Virginia put a plate with a neat slice of perfect rich fruitcake in front of them both. Robert Rowbottom looked irritably at Alison.

"Well, this letter. I can see that your property includes the right of parking on my drive for access to the rear of your property for maintenance and loading and unloading and so forth, but it really is damned annoying when I've set off down my lower drive on my way to an appointment and I'm delayed by something like an infernal builder's truck and have to stop my vehicle, find the driver and spend valuable time trying to get the obstacle out of the way in order to proceed on my own property!"

He picked up his fruit cake and munched. Alison broke off a piece of cake and nibbled. She let the silence stretch.

"The point is, my garage is round the back here. My four-wheel drive which I use when I go shooting is round the back here. I load up the kit and the dogs round the back and I drive out, when I wish to, along my lower drive. I am not prepared to drive down my lower drive, find it blocked by an infernal builder's truck and have to reverse all the way back up it again. What do you expect me to do? Ask for your permission? Telephone you and say is my lower drive blocked and if it is, when might it be free for me to drive along it? And coming home, am I to chance it, coming along the lane and then find I have to go all the way back to the main road and come up the front drive? Well? What's your answer to that?" He leaned aggressively towards her, big hands on the table; fingers stretched over the oilcloth and enunciated her name deliberately. "Alison."

"I do see your point absolutely." Alison was earnest. "And of course for me, I will need access to the rear of my property for the delivery of things such as plants and compost and maybe roofing materials or painting equipment, all the things required to keep a property in good order. And that is what I will be doing, keeping this property in good order, which is actually to your advantage, do you not think? I mean, you'd hardly be pleased if you had a ramshackle building right on your lower drive, would you? It could have such an impact on Highvale House, to have The Stables deteriorating."

"This is a different issue," barked Robert Rowbottom. "Of course you will maintain The Stables. This village is in a conservation area and we all undertake to do our duty with the upkeep of our properties and the observance of things like tree preservation orders. But I am not prepared to be inconvenienced by obstruction on my property. Your letter," he stabbed a finger in the direction of the letter, "does not give you that permission. You do not have that right. Betty Morris never caused this trouble."

"Well frankly that doesn't surprise me. Have you seen the state of the backyard? There's a lot to be done to get it into order, I can tell you. Would it be acceptable to you if I tell you when I'm expecting a delivery? I know deliveries don't always arrive smack on time, but I expect this to be a temporary situation, just while I get things into order, and if I could telephone you to say when I expect a delivery perhaps the problem could be avoided."

Robert Rowbottom finished his cake.

"In fact," Alison smiled at him, "I was rather hoping to ask for your advice about where one can find things like reasonably priced compost for the garden and logs for my wood-burning stove." Careful, she thought, as she watched the man across the table from her settle down, don't get cocky. He may have a tendency to be a bully but he's not stupid and will notice if I try to manipulate him.

Robert Rowbottom pushed back his chair and stood. "In the interest of good neighbourliness we," he indicated his wife, "will of course give you any assistance we are able to. You have a right to load and off-load on my lower drive. That is not a right to park for prolonged periods. I would appreciate you letting me know when you are blocking my lower drive." He nodded and left the room as a car pulled up outside the back door.

"That'll be Maggie," said Virginia. "She helps me in the house." The dogs barked wildly. The door opened and Maggie arrived, firmly greeting the dogs and pointing to their baskets.

"Hiya," she said, bag down, coat off, boots shed and light canvas indoor shoes slipped onto her feet almost before her greeting was out. "I'm Maggie." She smiled at Alison.

"Maggie, meet Alison Henderson. Alison, this is Maggie Scutter."

"Pleased to meet you," said Maggie. "So, where shall I start today?" She turned to Virginia. "Anyone coming this weekend?"

"I should go," Alison stood up. "You have things to do. Thank you for the tea, Virginia, and please tell Mr Rowbottom that I will take great care to tell him about all that's going on at The Stables."

"Oh, you're the one who's just moved into Betty's place are you? Nice there, isn't it? Need any help? I've got a couple of hours spare."

"Maggie, come on." Virginia laughed. "How can you possibly have any time free, what with the girls and your home-care job and all the extras?"

"Well, I like to keep busy. So, where shall I start today?"

ALISON TURNED up her collar as she walked down the drive between the lime trees and pushed her hands deep into her pockets. Well, that seemed very satisfactory. Live and let live. Better to be sure to let Rowbottom know if I need to use his drive. So that's the next thing, then. Get this garden sorted. She'd almost reached the gate when yet another vehicle arrived at Highvale House, this time turning into the gateway and revving as it raced into the drive. Alison's hands were out of her pockets, arms flailing as she overbalanced in her leap to get out of the way and she hurtled into the trunk of a tree, sliding awkwardly down it and finishing in a heap on the dry leaves at its base.

The vehicle stopped in a flurry of gravel and the window slid down. Alison heard the quiet throb of the powerful engine and her own breath quietening as her panic subsided. The driver leaned across the passenger seat and watched her stand up awkwardly, brush at the leaves which clung to her, and toss her hair off her face. He leaned further towards the window and rested his arm along the car door.

"I would not have believed it possible." The voice was measured and masculine, an edge of roughness and a promise of power but with a tone of mildly surprised boredom. The square face, immaculately clean shaven, had a weathered look. There was no hint of a smile.

They looked at one another with recognition.

"Do you never look where you're going? Can you not hear when a car is approaching?" His unblinking gaze travelled from the top of her head down her pale camel coat to her shiny designer boots standing in the leaf litter. "You're a townie, aren't you? Well, someone should have told you that it's safest to walk on the side of the road facing the oncoming traffic and you should be alert at all times, looking and listening. There are very few pedestrian pavements here, you know. Presumably you can walk and I don't have to heave you aboard and take you anywhere?" The bored voice ceased and one eyebrow was raised as he waited for an answer.

Alison was speechless at the total lack of concern for someone he could have injured. In disgust, she steadied herself and resisted the impulse to brush the leaves off her coat. With her head held high, and without looking back she set off silently down the drive, through the gate and out into the lane, taking care in the gathering dusk to walk on the side of the road facing the oncoming traffic. As she did so, she furiously blinked back tears. Tears of frustration, she told herself, frustration and anger. Who is that incredibly rude man? Here am I trying to manage all on my own and I seem to have nothing but obstacles and problems and difficult people to deal with. Perhaps she'd made a terrible mistake in moving after all.

Alison's self doubt and sudden vulnerability following her encounters at Highvale House infuriated her. All her feelings of rejection, so carefully sorted out and tidied away, swooped back and inhabited her, smothering feelings of well-being, diminishing her self-esteem and denting her new independent persona; the cheerful, competent, content Alison. Gone was her sense of adventure, her drive to carve out a new life. Mechanically she went through the motions of responding to minutiae. She spoke with her sisters on the phone, her voice bright and brittle as she forced herself to give a positive picture of life in Highvale, her lovely new house, her plans for the garden, the dispatch of the inhabitants of her attic and the triumphant chiming of her beautiful clock bringing the voice of The Stables alive again.

She paid her newspaper bill at the shop, wrote to friends in gratitude for thoughtful housewarming gifts of flowers, a little gardening book, an amusing tea towel. She fed the birds, taking care with the amount of bird food she put out and carefully sweeping the small area outside the kitchen window late each afternoon. When Ed phoned with a plea for help when their planned childcare failed at the last moment, it was almost with relief that she agreed to drive down to Hampshire the following day.

She packed her small overnight bag with essentials and dressed in jeans, shirt, fleece and trainers, grabbed a bottle of wine from the fridge and headed for Hampshire.

"Alison you're a lifesaver," Giselle ushered her into the house. "It's really good of you to come at such short notice. We just had to be in London for the opening of this exhibition. This is my biggest chance yet to really get G H Interiors on the map. Toby and Chloe know you're collecting them from school." She swept Alison into the exquisite house, furnished as a showcase for Giselle's interior design company. All was light; huge windows, glass tables, vast mirrors, pale furniture, a startling expanse of wallpaper in one area, and strategically placed objects and accent colours in another. Alison was grateful on her grandchildren's behalf that they had a playroom and a secluded back garden to be untidy in.

"Usual bedroom, Giselle?"

"Yes. Dump your bag and I'll put the kettle on and fill you in." Over a mug of coffee in the immaculate kitchen Giselle gave instructions about the collection of the children from school, Chloe's music practice, the requirements of homework, supper and bedtime. "And you know Toby will try to charm you into letting him stay up," she finished.

"Well I hope he'll try," said Alison wryly, "a little charm can be very pleasant."

Giselle looked at her astutely. "That doesn't sound like you. Problems?"

"Oh not really. Just a bit uphill at the moment. No, I mean it. A little charm can go a long way and I love the way Toby tries it on. Don't worry. He won't succeed." She smiled, touched that the utterly focussed Giselle had even noticed the tiny downturn of her tone. "All will be well and I have your mobile number. Away you go and get ready. I've brought you a bottle of pink bubbly to toast the success of G H Interiors. I'll put it in the fridge."

ALISON HOVERED in the school playground waiting for the children, glad to be among the young parents and au pairs doing the same. She checked in with the teachers and had delighted hugs from Chloe and, in front of his friends, a more restrained greeting from Toby. The chatter of the children, the piling into the house, dropping bags and coats, both talking nonstop at the same time, grabbed her attention and she gave herself up to their needs, moving into their world of fish fingers, not too much ketchup, finish your milk, who's feeding the hamster, and have you finished your homework?

"I've got reading," said Chloe.

"How lovely. Bring your book and read to me. I love being read to." They cosied up in the playroom and Chloe successfully completed her reading.

"I like reading to you, Granny. What do you like doing?"

"Well, I like listening to you reading."

"But you can't do that in your new house because I'm not there. What do you like doing in your new house, Granny?"

Alison was silent. There didn't seem to be anything she liked doing, only things which must be done.

"Well, I like watching the birds which come to my bird feeder and I like walking along the pretty lane outside my house to the village shop."

Chloe was unimpressed, her big eyes unblinkingly regarding her grandmother. "Is that all?" she asked.

"Well, I've been very busy moving in to the new house and there's lots to be done when you move. There's unpacking and clearing away all the boxes and putting things in cupboards and hanging up the curtains. Lots. The next thing I have to do is the garden."

"Can I come and help you in the garden?"

"I would love that, darling. I'll tell you all about what we need to plant and what it will look like in the summer. Jake will help me with the digging, but you could come with me to buy the plants. What d'you think?"

"Ooh yes. Shall we have flowers and tomatoes?"

"Good idea. Now, what about bathtime?"

DRIVING HOME THE NEXT DAY, Giselle's excitement about her success at the exhibition stayed with Alison for some time. She was pleased for her; pleased that her daughter-in-law had found an outlet for her creativity which she managed to fit in with her family responsibilities. She felt tired but refreshed by her contact with the family and as she neared Highvale her fingers gripped the steering wheel tighter and she resolved to pull herself together and be able to give Chloe a better answer next time she said, 'what do you like doing, Granny?'

Home again and through her front door she stepped on a piece of paper, picked it up and took it into the kitchen, turning it over in her hand. It was a narrow slip of printed paper with a small watercolour printed on one side and on the other, now decorated with the imprint of her trainer, an invitation to an exhibition in the Village Hall.

'COUNTRY LANDSCAPES. PAINTINGS IN WATER-COLOUR BY AIDAN FORESTER.'

She put the announcement on her fridge door, securing it with a bright magnetic strawberry. She would go.

THE VILLAGE HALL was past the shop on the edge of the Green.

Outside was a glass-fronted noticeboard filled with information about the Scouts, the Women's Institute, yoga classes, rubbish collection, a lost cat, curtain-making services and a toddler group. Maybe not quite my thing, thought Alison. She collected her newspaper and milk and then called in at the Village Hall. Wearing a dark quilted jacket, warm cord trousers and robust boots, she was amused to notice that she was at least beginning to look more like a villager as she joined the few people who were wandering about the hall looking at the pictures. There were paintings of fields and woodlands, barns and cowsheds, the village church and the pond. Then her heart leapt. She saw her Stables, her silver birches over the wall, her blue and white clock on the old slate roof and her green door with the joyful bell beside it. She loved the loose way in which it was painted, the impressionistic suggestion of the birches, the light which glanced off their pale slender branches. She loved the hint of shine on the roof, as though it had rained; the darkness of the shadow under the clock tower and defining the door in the wall. The picture was well drawn, the colours clear and fresh and the whole subject presented with a nonchalant elegance and confidence. She took a deep breath and heard her breath echoed behind her.

"Intake of breath. Big sigh. Something you like? Something you don't like!" She stepped back and trod on a battered cowboy boot, throwing herself momentarily off balance before being steadied against the languid frame of Aidan Forester, one of her hands clutching his unzipped fleece, the other gripping his striped scarf which tightened round his neck until he gently untangled her and, with hands on her shoulders, ensured her firm footing.

"Oh I'm so sorry. I didn't hear you come up behind me."

"No apology required. The customer must always be taken care of and I rather hope you might be one. A customer. You seem to like this picture." His head was inclined as he looked down at her, eyes focussed disarmingly on Alison. "Would you like me to tell you about it?" She nodded. Placing his hand under her elbow, he drew her back from the picture and positioned her at his chosen distance, his hand remaining under her elbow, keeping her close to him. As he talked, she could feel his voice as well as hear it, flowing, articulate and full of different sound, now fast, now slow, as he described how he felt about the scene before him, what he was trying to convey and how he'd used the paint. Alison was fascinated.

"So this wasn't about being decorative, finding a pretty scene and transferring it to paper?"

"Heavens no," Aidan smiled as he looked down at her and released her from his gentle but far from fleeting grasp, putting his hands in his pockets. "It's what I feel that drives me to paint and my endeavour is to communicate to you," one hand moved from his pocket to lightly touch Alison's shoulder, "what I feel." His hand rested on his chest. He smiled, hands back in his pockets. Neither spoke. Alison recovered her composure.

"So what do you hope you've made me feel about this building, this scene?" She waved her hand vaguely in the direction of the picture.

"Well, I should be asking you what it's saying to you."

"I know what it's saying to me and I asked you first."

"OK then. What appealed to me was the way the building sits in its environment, settled in, as it were, part of the landscape with a right to be there, as though it grew there with the trees that are in close proximity and those at a distance behind it. I liked the closeness of the lane to the wall, giving the building an accessibility that makes it part of the community. I also like the way it clearly had one use and now has another, was a stables and now is a dwelling and I think that adds to its charm, that as a building it's too valuable to discard and once a certain use is no longer viable, it can adapt to another use. I like that. The adaptability. To change as needs must but also because you want to. And I like the juxtaposition of that rather

grand and beautifully proportioned clock in its cupola, on the
roof of such a practical building. That amuses me."

Alison wasn't looking at the picture. She was giving Aidan
her rapt attention as he put into words all that she herself felt.
They looked at one another silently until he asked, "Not
impressed? Faintly bored, perhaps."

"Oh no. No, no, no. Not at all," Alison's words stumbled
out. Aidan smiled.

"Good. So when painting this, I wanted to keep it light and
loose, unpretentious if you like, so you have the sort of feeling
you get from the smell of new baked bread or autumn leaves
on a bonfire, special and totally of itself but also an everyday
sort of feeling that comforts when you see it. There's coffee to
be had at the other end of the hall. Does the idea appeal?"

Alison nodded and was shepherded to a table, gratefully
subsiding into a plastic chair and letting her bag with her newspaper and milk slide to the floor as she accepted a cup of
coffee. She gave herself up to Aidan's relaxed attention, agreed
to buy the painting, gave him her phone number and her
address.

"Well hello," he said, reading it, "I knew the new owner
had arrived at The Stables and I'm so pleased to meet you.
Now, was it fair to let me go banging on about your house not
knowing who you were?"

"Well yes. I think so. Because your opinion was thus totally
honest and I'm truly stunned because your feelings about my
house completely echo my own." She stopped, faintly embarrassed. She did not normally delve into the subject of feelings
with someone of such short acquaintance. Oh don't be so
stuffy, she said to herself. Just enjoy the moment.

"Interesting. And do you think I've managed to capture
what you feel?" He leant back in his chair, smiling, waiting.

"Yes I do. It's quite an odd feeling, really, I mean, your
painting sort of sharing my feelings."

"Would I be right if I said you've been having a lot of, shall we say feeling, to be getting a grip of lately?"

Alison was startled, unwilling to go any further. "Well, moving is usually a fairly stressful activity, wouldn't you say?" She began to briskly gather her bag and her jacket.

Aidan remained still, watching her. "Have you ever painted?"

"I've dabbled, you know, just for fun. I used to work in a drawing office, for a map publisher, before I was married." Her voice tailed off.

Aidan leant forward, his hands on the table between them. "Tell you what. Come and join my class. It's a good way to meet people and painting is unbeatable for sorting out those feelings." He smiled and briefly clasped her hand, almost instantly releasing it.

"Here. This is my number and these are the times and places of the class. Beginners welcome and a glass in the pub at the end of our efforts. Call me if you're interested."

Before she reached home she knew she'd do it. That's what I need, something that is not required of me, not a practical necessity but just for fun. I shall dabble in some painting just for fun. And her spirits lifted as she stored away the thought of fun and prepared herself for the arrival of Jake the gardener.

5

It was raining when Jake arrived but he was not a guy to be daunted by the weather and cheerfully shook off his jacket and discarded his boots in the hall.

"Hi there. Good to see you. Now, how do you want to play this?"

"Well, I'm a total novice, so I'll listen to you. Shall we have coffee and talk about it?"

"Sure." Jake put his hand in the pocket of his combat trousers and pulled out a tea bag. "Rooibos tea. Good stuff." He smiled and handed it to Alison.

"No problem. Go through the sitting room to the big window at the end. We can talk there where we can see the garden."

JAKE DRANK his Rooibos and surveyed the bedraggled garden in silence. Alison, dressed in tracksuit and sweater, ready to lend a hand, observed him. He was lean and angular with capable hands, stubble on his bony jaw, an almost shaven head and an interesting variety of ear and facial ornaments adorning his piercings – a silver stud, a tiny skull, a yin and yang motif, a crucifix on a minute chain. He screwed up his green eyes as he looked first to one side of the stable yard and then the other, turning his head slowly, taking it all in. Alison looked too, waiting for him to speak.

The bricks of the old wall enclosing the yard were shaded pinks and oranges, some dusted with chalkiness. In one corner they looked grey with damp and in places were draped with discoloured, bedraggled vegetation. The coping on top of the wall was damaged in places and a square coping stone was missing beside the door at the end. The large pale buff flag-stones which haphazardly covered the ground were well worn, puddled with rainwater in places, lying unevenly in others, reflecting fragments of sky. In the middle of the yard was the brick roundel where her interest in making a garden here had first quickened. She looked at the desiccated mess of spent vegetation within it and found herself really interested to know what the plants were. She remembered smelling mint, but who knew what other lovely herbs might be there.

"Before I say what I think, what do you want from your garden?" Jake spoke without looking at her, his attention on the stable yard.

"I hadn't really thought. I mean, I don't know what options I might have."

"OK. Forget the thinking. What do you feel? What might you want to feel when you're in the garden? What can you see yourself doing?"

"Well, off the top of my head, I'd like to sit somewhere to have coffee and stuff and, oh yes, there's that rather ramshackle gazebo thing over there. I wondered if that was somewhere which would be pleasant in the early evening, perhaps at sunset, maybe to watch the sun go down if I could see it from there? Have a glass of wine? And I'd like to pick fresh herbs, things like mint and parsley and basil."

"OK. That's all a good start. What might you like to see? Abundant rambling roses and honeysuckle spilling their scent about the place or neat clipped lollipops of holly and little box hedges? Organic veggies and a haven for wildlife?" Jake put down his mug and smiled at her. Alison felt unsure.

"I really don't know. I think if you suggest what you think may grow well here, I'll go along with that. It's only a small garden, after all, and I think it should be in keeping with the building. This is not a grand building, as you see, and I like its practical workaday origins and wouldn't want to pretty it up, if you know what I mean."

"I absolutely do and couldn't agree with you more. A garden has its own spirit, its own sense of place and it's important to identify that. It's good if you can walk into a garden and say yes, there is a definite feeling of character here; this is a unique and living thing and it works. A garden can transmit a feeling to you, can excite you or calm you, energise you or encourage you to drift and dream." Jake was looking at her intently, green eyes smiling, head on one side waiting for her reply.

"I had no idea there was all that to it. So what you're saying is, this is a sort of partnership. We identify some elements I'd like to have but we listen to what the house and the space might also want?"

"Got it in one. I wish all my clients would listen to the space and not try to impose grand or crazy ideas on their gardens. Still, they say the customer's always right, don't they, and sometimes the craziest ideas are the most expensive, so who am I to complain? OK. Here's the plan."

Jake pulled a pad and pencil from his shirt pocket. "I'm going to jot down here the way I think we should do things and it would be good if you made a list too so we both know where we're at. First I'll take a good look at what's here and suggest what should go, what you might keep and what needs renovating. I'll check out the walls for any repairs and we'll need to think of hard landscaping, you know, where your coffee area will be and that stuff. The flagstones in the yard will need a bit of attention too." He stopped as Alison held up her hand.

"Sorry to interrupt you, but there are flagstones with deep ruts. I love the ruts, you know, where some cart or carriage or something used to come in and out of the yard. I wouldn't want those changed in any way." Jake made a note.

"Gotcha. Won't do a thing without your permission. Right," he stuffed the pad and pencil back in his pocket, "a survey then. I'll do a thorough survey and let you have that and then, with your agreement, I can crack on." He walked back to the hall.

"There is just one thing." Alison followed him. "I have access into the yard from my neighbour's drive at the back there and it's a bit of a sensitive issue. I can't block his drive and I have agreed to inform him when there's loading and unloading going on."

Jake smiled, sorting out his boots. "Understood." He grunted as he pulled on a boot, "Plenty of notice, then. There'll be manure and compost needed, building materials, timber, concrete, the mixer and then of course the plants." He shrugged on his jacket and smiled at Alison. "Don't look so anxious. I'm a sensitive guy. I won't upset your neighbour and I'll try to co-ordinate deliveries so we minimise disruption."

Alison put a hand on the sleeve of his jacket with grateful relief. "Oh thank you. That is thoughtful and I'm so grateful. It's been a bit of a nightmare to be honest, and what with me being new here I feel I haven't got off to a very good start. My neighbour's been really annoyed and quite unpleasant."

"No worries. I'll get some kit out of my van and walk round the back. Door unlocked?"

"I'll do it now."

. . .

JAKE WAS WELL into his survey when Alison was surprised by the jangle of her front-door bell. It was Virginia Rowbottom with dogs on their leads held with one hand and clutching something with the other which she held out to Alison. Alison took the offering and Virginia tied the dogs to the gate post, commanding "Sit!" and pointing to the ground with her hand. The dogs sat.

"Hello Alison." Virginia smiled. "Walking the dogs and thought I'd call on you and bring you this."

"How lovely. Will they be alright if you come in?"

"Absolutely. Stay," she commanded again and followed Alison into the house, slipped off her boots and hung up her jacket.

"Oh what a delightful little kitchen. So smart. And so tidy. I try hard to be tidy and it never seems to happen."

"But your kitchen is wonderful," protested Alison, "warm and embracing and obviously busy too. You clearly enjoy cooking. Oh and how lovely this looks." Alison unwrapped a fat jar with a bright fabric cover on its lid and a label with Highvale House Pickled Pears clearly written on it. "I shall so enjoy this. I'm hopeless at this sort of thing. I tried to make marmalade once and when he tasted it my husband said it would work better with cold meat than on toast." She smiled at Virginia and put the jar down on the shiny granite surface. "I'll make some coffee. Come and see round my house." She had noticed Virginia pick up the mention of a husband. Might as well clear the decks, she thought.

"I'm divorced," she said, pouring the coffee. "The years of travelling came to an end but my husband, James," she hesitated, "my ex-husband, suddenly found someone else who, funnily enough, was about to start travelling so off he went, to be a trailing spouse. Ironic, don't you think?" She knew how brittle her voice sounded but telling Virginia seemed to create an intimacy between them which comforted her.

"I'm glad you told me. Hard to do?" Virginia offered no comment and her instant interest in Alison's immediate feelings was kind and heartwarming.

Alison nodded. "Surprisingly hard. You're the first stranger, if you like, I've explained my situation to. I mean, it's different with close friends and family. The word gets about somehow, you know, and everyone expresses the first thing they think; poor you, what a bastard, that sort of thing. But it happened and here I am and you can only take so much pity and sympathy. So, I'm starting again and actually I'm finding the challenge enjoyable. Maybe enjoyable is not quite the word! Stimulating, perhaps. I don't mean to sound like 'the plucky little woman', but these are my own challenges and although being on your own is without doubt alarming at times, and there are inevitably low times, I really think I'm lucky to have what I have. Now, let me show you round the house. I've got Jake here today, too. Starting on the garden."

"Well if you're going to be working on the garden, perhaps you could do with some help in the house? Maggie was serious, you know. Asked me to tell you. She used to help Betty out. She could give you a couple of hours a week."

By the time Virginia left Alison had agreed to talk to Maggie and arrangements had been made for the painting class.

"I'll tell Aidan you're coming. You can bring your cheque with you then and this is what he likes us to have." She wrote a list which Alison read with delight. A sketchbook, HB pencil, rubber, pad of not cold pressed watercolour paper, number 4, number 7 and number 10 watercolour brush, 13mm flat brush, a medium wash brush and a small tin of watercolours. "And why don't you come round for kitchen supper tonight. Just family. Seven-ish. Come up the lower drive. It's shorter."

In moments, Virginia was into her boots and untying her dogs and was dragged energetically down the lane.

. . .

JAKE SHOWED her his roughly drawn preliminary plan.

"So here we have the points of the compass, and this is the roundel in the middle of the yard, so you see the space can be quartered with one line from the house to the door in the back wall there and another from side to side, from the gazebo in this position here. You could have a nice toolshed on the opposite side, so you get these four paths with the roundel at the centre. And yes, you were quite right, you'll be able to see the sun set from the gazebo. Shouldn't take too much work to make it secure and its age does lend some charm, don't you think? A venerable gazebo!"

"What do you think about the old flagstones?"

"The flagstones are great and just need re-laying in places and it's not a problem to get more from a reclaim yard so you can have an interesting interface between old and new. I think filling in spaces with gravel would work well too. Plants readily self seed in gravel so you would soon have the edges softened. My idea is to give the space a strong form, good bones, if you like, with this plan and some structural planting, and then to soften it with more informal plants which could give you seasonal colour too. We'd need some bricks to repair parts of the wall. Should be able to get them from the reclaim company too."

"And where do you see my little morning area?"

"We could add some more flagstones here so you come out of these doors straight onto a little terrace. I though a pretty ornamental tree would be good here, give you seasonal interest and some dappled shade. Come outside with me and you can envisage the plan in situ."

They walked round the bedraggled old yard, muddy and puddled, its dejected plants drooping in the damp cold, fallen bricks and loose planks jumbled at the base of a wall, a small heap of builders' rubble with a paint can on top and an ancient metal watering can lying on its side obstructing the path. Alison, eyes now opened to both the potential and the challenge of her stable yard, stopped and took a deep breath. "Well, I can see you've got your work cut out."

"Not me. We. This is your garden. This must reflect you, be part of your personal creativity. Otherwise it'll have no soul, just be a showpiece. You still have to consider whether you want a greenhouse, a vegetable plot and where your compost bins will be. And finally, wildlife."

"Wildlife? Whatever do you mean? We're planning a garden here, not a safari park?"

"Gardens are shared places and many small creatures benefit plants as well, admittedly, as destroying them! But it's all about balance; about encouraging the beneficial creatures and discouraging those which may do harm. We'll let nature help us."

"I'm in your hands, Jake. I can see this is going to be a steep learning curve. Time for a coffee before you go?"

They kicked off their boots and the big glass door closed behind them. Jake held out his hand. "Rooibos tea," he said, passing her his teabag.

She laughed. "Sorry. Forgot. Sit over there at the table. You see I got some gardening magazines? My homework."

"I HOPE you don't mind me asking this, Jake," said Alison, putting his mug in front of him. He looked at her with narrowed eyes, a smile on his thin face as she paused, pulling out a chair and sitting down, pushing aside the magazines, putting her mug on the table, "but you're such an intriguing enigma. What did you do before you did your gardening course? Don't answer that if you don't want to."

"Well, this is a complete life change for me and I really love it. I've done all sorts of stuff, much of which you wouldn't want to know about. I did an electronics degree when I was younger and then for quite a while I was a roadie with rock bands. Great life. Interesting stuff. I've been all over the world, met all sorts of people, but suddenly it seemed right to stop the wandering and get settled, you know, put down some roots."

"Is that why you chose to do this?"

"It was a question of what will I enjoy doing and where do I want to live and which is more important, the place or the occupation. I found the occupation first. I love working outside, the physical effort required and turning my hand to anything – a bit of carpentry, some work with concrete, planting, cultivating, getting the soil right. And then I have to use my brain too, with the design and planning and," he leaned forward and prodded the table with his forefinger, "I have to do my own accounting and marketing and all that interface with the customer stuff."

"And then you found the place?"

"Then I found the girl and she was in the place!"

"Aah. That makes sense. I hope you don't think I was prying, and I do know what you mean about putting down roots."

"Is that what you're doing?"

"Do you know, I think maybe it is. What I'm trying to do, anyway. But you can't tell at once, can you? I mean, people thrive in their own element, don't they? You were talking about the balance needed for wildlife to flourish, creatures in their element with all that they need, food, shelter, security. It seems strange to be saying this at my age, but I'm not really sure what my element is, whether it's town or country, solitude or togetherness. Who knows. I'll find out, won't I?"

"Have you ever thought of doing yoga? Patti, my partner, does yoga classes. And meditation."

"Well, to be honest, I don't think that's really me, and I've just signed up for a painting class, so with that and the garden I think I'll be well occupied. But thank you for the thought."

BY THE TIME Jake left Alison felt the beginning of contentment, a satisfaction with the ordinary things of life she had not felt for some time. The transformation of the garden interested her and Virginia's informal and friendly visit had been comforting. Oh the pleasure of ordinary things, she thought, ordinary, domestic things. But maybe I really am getting a grip on this haven of mine, on my life. And that, she found, was another small pleasure. She was making her own choices and hopefully they would be the right ones. And she felt confident that as her experience of making the right choices increased so would her feelings of vulnerability diminish. For that was her ultimate goal. Invulnerability.

6

That evening, Alison dressed in narrow chocolate trousers, a fine wool lime-green top and a soft buttermilk suede jacket, loosely tying back her hair. She finished her simple makeup with coral lipstick and the faintest flourish of her favourite scent. She left The Stables in pleasant anticipation, leaving a light shining across the stable yard, and shone her way along the lower drive of Highvale House with her torch. Now, do I go to the front or the back door? Virginia said kitchen supper. Informal. She chose the back and, negotiating her way round a large black four-wheel-drive vehicle, rapped on the door. She shone her torch again on the vehicle. It was a Traiblazer. Was it the one she'd encountered before? It was too dark to be sure.

"Alison, hello. Welcome. Come in." Virginia opened the door and the dogs leapt up to contribute their greeting. Alison waited, smiling, while Virginia commanded the dogs. "The men will join us in a minute; just Robert and David, my brother-in-law. Grab a chair. White wine?"

As Virginia poured, Alison heard voices down the long tiled hall.

"Not a snowball in hell's chance. I remember when he was Station Commander he had these crazy ideas and who can say why he hung on as long as he did." The masculine voice was measured, the impression of carefully contained power tempering the edge of roughness. She felt nervous. It was the man who had been so rude and had so infuriatingly reduced her to tears. The Trailblazer driver was Virginia's brother-in-law David Rowbottom. She gathered her resources and prepared to be icily polite; please not another confrontation.

She smiled her thanks as Virginia put a glass of cold white wine on the kitchen table in front of her and returned to the Aga, moving pans and opening and shutting the oven door. Alison sipped her wine, hearing fragments of the conversation down the hall. Well she wasn't surprised, really, that the rude man was Robert Rowbottom's brother. Discourtesy clearly ran in the family. She heard footsteps in the hall and Robert Rowbottom filled the doorway into the kitchen.

"Hello Alison." He came towards her. Behind him came a man propelling himself in a wheelchair. "David, this is Alison Henderson."

"Hello," she said, stunned. She found herself blushing as she tried to quench the look of surprise which she knew had flooded her face, but her feeling of dislike for this discourteous man was not so easy to mask. She saw his look of exasperated recognition before he came towards her, lifted a hand off the arm of his wheelchair and, taking her hand briefly in his, swiftly released it.

"Hi there," he said as he expertly manoeuvred the wheel-chair to the opposite side of the table. "I'd better keep out of your way, city dweller. Got the table between us and my brakes on, so we should be safe, don't you think?" He regarded her without a smile.

She took her time to reply. "The phrase that springs to my mind is 'wide berth'. Perhaps if we agree to give one another a wide berth we could avoid any further unfortunate close encounters. Or maybe wide berth is too naval. Is there an aeronautical equivalent?"

There was complete silence as David and Alison looked steadily at one another. Even the dogs were still. A pan boiled over. Virginia rushed to the rescue.

"You've met before?" Robert passed his brother a glass of beer.

"Well, met is hardly the word. As, er, Alison has said, encountered is more like it. Anyway, it's good to be here and supper smells great, Virginia." He dismissed his encounters with Alison. She watched him as he talked, his broad shoulders moving as he changed position restlessly in the wheelchair, his strong capable hands on the table as he picked up a spoon, emphasised a point he was making, put down his glass. Not once did he glance in her direction. Not once did he acknowledge her presence. His shirt collar was crisp under his square jaw; his thick hair neatly cut and she noticed the tightening movement of a small muscle in his cheek when he listened. He addressed not a word to her. She was rattled by his discourtesy. Two could play at that game. She turned to his brother.

"Robert," she gave him the benefit of her most dazzling smile, asked him about his day, his dogs, his shooting, his activities with village organisations, his politics, his life. Years of diplomatic dinners and embassy cocktail parties had honed her skills to an impressive level and Robert Rowbottom buckled under the onslaught of her charm and sincerity. All semblance of his commanding-officer attitude melted. He responded with warmth and gave her his undivided attention with a monologue about his passion for country pursuits and the sheer idiocy displayed by those wanting to change age-old traditions which had successfully managed the country for generations. Alison's knowledge of such things was zero, but she appreciated his passion and felt his intention was good. Across the table from her, David listened silently.

"Are you not interested in country pursuits, David?" Alison asked, rattled by his silence. As she finished her question, looking into his unsmiling face, she realised her mistake. The wheelchair. How could she! "Oh I'm so sorry. How stupid of me." She flushed.

"Stupid is not the word which springs immediately to mind. But no, I'm not interested in country pursuits. Rob always was, even as a boy. But not me. Flying was the only thing that ever interested me." He turned away. "So Virginia, tell us about the girls. How are they doing?"

Dismissed again, thought Alison. Well clearly there's very little point in me even trying to communicate with him in a civil way. Alison lifted her chin defiantly, masking her sneaking feeling of pettiness.

Virginia's lasagne and tossed salad, plum and almond crumble with crème fraiche and some good cheddar to finish were much appreciated and were it not for the awkwardness with David, Alison would have loved the evening.

"I must go," she said at last. "This has been so nice, Virginia. Thank you. I've really enjoyed being with you all."

She stood up, smiling, thanked Robert for her coat, and extracted her torch from her pocket. David moved towards the back door.

"I'll drop you off. My car's outside."

"That won't be necessary." She was unsmiling, buttoning her coat.

"Oh come now, Alison," Robert interrupted, "we can't possibly let you walk home in the dark. Please let David see you home."

· · ·

RELUCTANTLY SHE CONSENTED and watched as David manoeuvred his wheelchair round the Trailblazer to the driver's side, hoisted himself in and expertly folded the wheelchair and stowed it behind the driver's seat. Robert ushered her into the passenger seat and closed the door as David gunned the engine into life. She was acutely aware of everything he did as he drove – how he handled the wheel, letting it slip lightly through his fingers; how he controlled the big vehicle, easily and commandingly, as if it were second nature. She was aware of the slight but distinctive fresh smell of what? His soap, aftershave? Spicy lime and sea spray. Ozone. Rain on new grass. Cool cucumber. Or was it somewhere between coriander and lavender? She looked straight ahead, as did he. She sat primly, her knees together, her torch held on her lap with both hands.

"Would you like me to drop you at your back gate or round at the front?"

"Just here at the back will be fine, thank you."

"I'll wait until I hear your door shut."

"There's no need for you to do that."

She opened the door and was out, turning to close it when he said, "As you wish," and, tapping the steering wheel with his fingers and gently revving his engine, he smiled at her. So engaging was his smile she almost returned it but just in time she slammed the door, opened her back gate, closing it with a firm click behind her and shone her way across the yard. The noise of the gently revving engine continued, soft in the background as she avoided the puddles and broken flagstones of the yard. With relief she opened the door to the house and as she closed it heard the briefest blast of a horn and the engine was released and roared into life. Not only did David have bad manners and a boorish attitude, he also couldn't take no for an answer. Wheelchair or not, manners maketh man, she thought. Would I tolerate the bad attitude if I knew why he needs a wheelchair? No. Why should I?

. . .

NEXT MORNING MAGGIE arrived in a whirl of practical efficiency, canvas shoes and rubber gloves on in no time and firing a fusillade of suggestions about the best cleaning materials, which bit to do first and how a J-mop was just the thing for the stairs which were a bugger to get right. She said she'd have a coffee when she'd finished upstairs and the bathrooms.

"Kellie-Ann will pick me up. She's using my car today," she said as she disappeared up the stairs. Maggie was small and lively, her rounded form squeezed into stretchy jeans and her hair stridently highlighted. The fleece she'd hung in the hall was an impressive shade of mauve and the boots she'd swapped for her canvas shoes were adorned with high heels and chains and buckles. Over coffee, Maggie told Alison about her husband, 'my Tone', who could turn his hand to anything. She talked about her three daughters and two granddaughters, all of whom lived with her, there being no partners, husbands or sweethearts at the moment, and her numerous jobs which included working for a Home Care agency.

"We go to David, too, when he needs us, me and Kellie-Ann. She works for the same agency. Serenity, it's called. Stupid name, don't you think? We never have time for no serenity. It's in, do what you have to and out again. But not with David, of course." Her face softened as she said his name.

"Why not with David?"

Maggie looked surprised. "Because it's David!" she said.

"So why do you go to David?"

"Oh I'm sorry. Not allowed to say. Client confidentiality." Maggie shook herself like a hen shaking and then settling its feathers. "Well, better get on. Kellie-Ann will be here before you know it."

. . .

They didn't hear Kellie-Ann tooting her mother's car horn and she was forced to pull the doorbell. When she opened the door, Alison saw a younger Maggie. Kellie-Ann's jet black hair was swept back into a ponytail and her orange fringe barely cleared her eyebrows. She had big hoop earrings and a nose stud, a bright red leather bomber jacket which stopped short of her slender midriff and jeans which looked sprayed on tucked into huge soft blue sheepskin boots collapsing round her ankles. She smiled warmly at Alison. Her pretty face was made up like a model's and a French manicure adorned her slender hands.

"Hi there. Come to get me Mum."

"Please come in. She won't be a moment. Your Mum tells me you work for a Care Agency."

"Yeah. Well, that's what I'm doing for now. I'm going to travel and the money's not bad if you do plenty of hours and work evenings and weekends. Next summer, I reckon I'll have enough and I'll be off. They keep saying they want me to do more training, you know for management and stuff, but I dunno. I mean, you got to do what you want while you're young. I look at our Donna, and there she is with two kids already and she's never travelled. Won't be doing it now, will she!" Kellie-Ann rattled the car keys, taking care not to damage her beautiful fingernails.

Maggie and Kellie-Ann stayed in Alison's head as she made her way to the art class. On a dull and chilly afternoon the sheer colourful exuberance of them both was a joy and encouraged her as she looked forward to the class and the challenge it presented. Virginia yoo-hooed from the other side of the room and she gratefully joined her, feeling like a new girl with her brand new kit.

"Hello Mrs Henderson, Alison," Aidan smiled his slow smile, "good to have you with us. I'll just get everyone started, if I may, and then you and I can have a chat so I can find out a bit about you and your art experience."

ALISON TOOK in her surroundings as Aidan started off his class. The small room in the Village Hall was well lit and arranged with big plastic folding tables and bright orange stacking chairs. There was a buzz of energy, people at the tables with smart art cases, plastic boxes or canvas bags of kit; small table-top easels, jam jars of water, collections of objects for still life, large and small pads of paper, rags and kitchen roll, an assortment of clearly vital things for each individual. And the individuals were as assorted as the equipment. There was a sleek-haired lady in a pastel fleece, an arty looking person in outsize garments of indeterminate colour, someone timid peering through large glasses apologetically sorting themselves out, jolly unselfconscious people with open smiles for whom enjoyment was clearly the priority, and the quiet, serious ones who were there to learn and improve their art.

"So, Alison," Aidan was by her side, "would you like to come over here to my table?" He held wide his arm, gesturing and escorting in one movement, and held her chair for her as she sat.

"Now, tell me about yourself and what your hopes might be, in terms of an art class." He sat back in his chair, elbows on the arms of the chair, hands together, fingertip to fingertip, focussing on her, waiting for her to speak. Alison leaned forward, hands gesturing as she spoke, that schoolgirl feeling creeping up on her again. She cleared her throat, unaccustomed to being a novice.

"Well, a long time ago I was a cartographer. I was fascinated by maps and travel, how areas were mapped and how maps were understood, and I learned draughtsman's skills and accuracy, especially with a mapping pen and ink. I used to sketch for fun and I've kept doing it now and then, when the mood took me or opportunity presented, but now I'd like to be able to draw better and to use paint. I've looked at paintings, in galleries and so on, and been to various lectures and the like, so I have reasonable background knowledge. I suppose I'd call it the average layperson's knowledge. But to be honest, I so love the picture you did of my house; it's quite inspirational. I like the way your painting looks like a mere suggestion of a building, yet the building is there in all its solidity. Magic. I don't expect to do be able to do it as well as you, of course, but I would like to try to do it as well as it's possible for me to do it." She stopped. There was silence. Aidan was regarding her intently. The silence lengthened. She looked at him enquiringly, raised her eyebrows, shifted in her chair.

"Has anyone ever told you your eyes are quite lovely? I could sit here all day looking at you and listening to you."

Alison flushed. Well, he was a painter. Presumably that was the sort of thing painters noticed or commented on.

"I don't think your idea would meet with the approval of the rest of the class," she said, glancing round the room, "and I'm not supposed to be doing the talking. Shouldn't I be listening to you?"

He sighed deeply. "Why is it that beautiful women are so often right?" Elegantly, he unfolded his tall frame and pushed back his chair. "OK. Back to the drawing board."

IT WAS GETTING dark outside and chairs were being stacked and tables folded and Alison was not ready to stop drawing.

"Time to go," said Virginia, "The Huntsman awaits."

"I just can't believe the time has gone so fast." Alison zipped up her pencil case, hastily packed away her stuff and dragged her chair to the stack. She joined Virginia at the door.

"One moment it was half past two and now it's dark. Amazing."

"It is, isn't it? That's apparently what using your right brain does. Creative things like drawing use your right brain. And you get totally absorbed. It's supposed to be really good for you. Good relaxation. Got your coat? Let's go."

In a few moments, the warmth of The Huntsman enfolded them and Alison was amused that now she was one of the flock of twittering sparrows she'd observed on her first night in Highvale. She settled on the edge of the flock, watching from the fringes as these good-natured and pleasant people finished off their creative afternoon with a glass of wine and a friendly exchange of views. And here was Aidan again, bottle in hand, pulling up a stool, squeezing in beside her. He topped up her glass and raised his own.

"Here's to art, and the art of living. Ah what is the art of living? Had I but a loaf of bread, a glass of good claret and thou, dear heart, I would be a happy man." He smiled. "And a hyacinth, of course."

"A hyacinth? You'd need a hyacinth too?"

"Of course a hyacinth. To feed the soul." He laughed pleasantly. "Come and have supper with me sometime. I make an interesting curry."

"Really?"

"Yup. I'll call you. OK?" He stood up, picked up his bottle and was gone from the fringe, back to his place by the bar.

WHEN SHE GOT HOME, Nick's van was outside The Stables and Nick was in the van.

"Mum, hi there," he was beside her giving her a hug, "where've you been?"

"I've been in the pub." She laughed, opening the door.

"Where have you been? Come in, come in. It's so nice to see you. I take it you'll be staying the night?"

"The pub? Life in the country driven you to drink, then?"

"Not at all. It's a long story. Come in and I'll fill you in."

She opened the door, put down her painting gear, clicked on lights, ushered him in. "Hang your coat there, Nick. It's a sandwich or something like that if you're hungry. We'll have a look in the fridge and forage." She jumped as the doorbell jangled, joyfully pealing into the night.

"Visitors at this hour, Mum?" Nick looked at her, smiling. "First the pub and now visitors. I'd say you've really arrived in the country."

"Nonsense." The bell jangled again and Alison opened the door. The glare of the outside light bouncing off her orange fringe, hoop earrings and slick little jacket, Kellie-Ann smiled her shiny lip-gloss smile.

"Hi there. All right? Me Mum left one of her shoes behind, you know, those canvas jobs she wears indoors? No, I won't come in," she said. "I've left the engine running."

"OK, Kellie-Ann. I'll get the shoe." Alison turned and found her way blocked by Nick, hands in pockets, leaning in the doorway. "Out of the way, Nick." She bustled past him and returned with the shoe, holding it out to Kellie-Ann.

"Thanks," Kellie-Ann reached out a twinkling manicured hand and took the shoe. "See ya." The other hand twinkled a wave and she was gone. Nick stood in the doorway, gazing down the lane looking at the space where she'd been.

Alison looked at him shrewdly. "Drop the latch when you close the door," she said.

7

Tousled and rumpled from sleep, Nick gratefully drank the coffee Alison poured him. "Haven't got long, Mum. Need to be up at Stafford by twelve-ish."

"That's fine. You've got time to give me a brief resume of your doings. How are things going?"

Over breakfast he spoke with enthusiasm about his work and recent events, then grabbed his bag, hugged his mother and was in his van and heading for Stafford.

FOR A WHILE AFTER NICK LEFT, the house felt very empty. He always had taken up all the available space, in the home and in her heart. His visit had reminded her of what had been her normality; the boys would come home and give their parents accounts of their lives, their friends, their joys and difficulties, always appreciating James' advice; always gratefully soaking up Alison's love and encouragement. She wondered how often she would see them, now James was no longer there. Or maybe they're in touch with him, she thought, surprised this hadn't occurred to her before. Maybe they're still getting that fatherly input. I don't think I really want to know, she thought. She wandered into her courtyard, thinking that however grown up one is, the breakup of a relationship inevitably has a fall-out. Maybe Nick's determined buoyancy did contain some bravado, for her sake. She really appreciated his effort. Still, he doesn't need nurturing anymore, she thought, but my plants do.

Jake had cleared the courtyard and re-pointed the walls, replacing some coping stones and cutting back all the creepers and climbers. There was a substantial new door in the wall, painted a soft dark teal blue with a big black wrought-iron ring as a handle. Beside it hung a bell like the one by the front door and on the wall each side of the door Jake had already fixed teal-washed trellising. The old flags had been re-laid and interspersed with reclaimed ones and gravel, a pattern of old bricks laid between them adding definition. In a corner away from the house was a neat blue shed and in the opposite corner, showing the beginnings of its refurbishment, the gazebo, her sunset hut.

In the middle of the courtyard stood the rebuilt roundel, the low circular brick wall neatly finished off with stone slabs and now full of soil and compost and ready for planting. At its centre, wooden trellising formed an obelisk waiting for the pretty clematis she'd chosen for this central herb bed. Against the wall stood a motley looking collection of plants in pots – mint and sage, rosemary, chives and thyme. Jake would be planting them on his next visit, giving them time to settle in before spring. But Jake expected Alison to plant the little thyme plants before then, tucking them randomly between the big flagstones in sunny spaces. Alison walked to the end of the courtyard, her thoughts taken over by climbing roses, small flowering cherry trees, foxgloves and cosmos, lavender and clipped bay. She turned and looked back at The Stables. It was all coming together in a very satisfactory way and she was enjoying learning about the plants, what they needed and the conditions they preferred. Her determination to learn was helping to soothe the part of her which still felt the pain of James' rejection; was beginning to fill the hollow James' abandonment had excavated within her. And there's more learning, too, she thought. The art lessons.

Aidan had seen the potential of her drawing from the moment she put pencil to paper. He urged her to draw every day if possible and offered extra tuition which she refused. But she had agreed to have supper with him and this evening she would be at his cottage at seven to try the curry he was so proud of. Meanwhile, she thought, there's all that thyme to plant. And she fetched her gardening gloves, kneeler and shiny new trowel from the shed and began choosing places for her plants.

Dusk was gathering when Alison stood back and looked round her courtyard, the flagstones softened now with the interspersed thyme, satisfied that Jake would approve. She gave them each some water then neatly put everything away and locked the shed. Just time for a quick mug of tea and then she would have to change. Suddenly Alison felt weary. All this determination and learning new stuff and meeting new people required so much energy. Maybe a hot shower and the tea would revitalize her.

It was a little after seven when Aidan opened the front door of his cottage. Light spilling out from the small windows was welcoming and she could smell the spices of the promised curry. Aidan, a tea towel over one shoulder and a much used apron wrapped around his tall frame, stood in the doorway gazing at her. Alison wore dark jeans, snakeskin pumps and a soft purple jacket over a crisp ivory shirt. She shifted the black shiny handbag which was slung over her shoulder and with a tinkle of thin gold bangles, tucked her hair behind her ear.

"May I leave my car just there?" she pointed.

Aidan jumped into action. "Oh yes. Yes of course. That's fine. Come in, come in." He held the door wide. "You look delightful." He shepherded her inside and closed the door. "D'you mind coming into the kitchen? I can talk to you there and do my finishing touches."

Alison walked into a scene of chaos so complete that not an inch of kitchen surface was visible. The sink was piled high with pans and utensils; bunches of dried herbs hung haphazardly from the low ceiling; a high cupboard door was open, revealing a jumble of jars of pickles, jams and sauce bottles. On a tray on the table stood an open bottle of wine in a terracotta cooler and two slender-stemmed glasses, delicately engraved.

"Here we are." Aidan pulled out a chair, flapping his tea towel at the seat, offering it to Alison. She sat, letting her shiny bag collapse on the floor and unbuttoning her jacket. Aidan poured a generous measure of wine into each glass and handed one to Alison. "This…" he raised his glass, held it to the light, twisted and slanted it, sipped some wine with a loud slurping noise and rolled it round his mouth, then swallowed and smiled. "Mmmm. This is the best chardonnay from the Barossa Valley. You need a good robust wine with spicy food, and to start we have vegetable pakoras, masala vada and my best chutneys to dip into."

He bent and pulled a large plastic laundry basket from under the table, swept some of the clutter off the table into it, and shoved the basket back underneath. Alison sipped the excellent wine and watched, amused. He pulled open a drawer and grabbed a bunch of assorted silver cutlery and placed it on the table, knives with ivory handles, fiddle pattern forks and spoons, a venerable pair of battered serving spoons. He lowered a Dutch airer from the ceiling, removed two blue-and-white-check napkins and re-hoisted the airer. "Voila. Table laid. How's the wine?"

He was across the kitchen stirring a pan with his back to her before she spoke. "It's lovely. How efficient you are in the kitchen." The irony was lost on him.

"Well, you know, man on his own. Needs must." He banged the spoon on the side of the pan and opened and shut the oven door. "I either learned to do it myself or never had anything delicious to eat. So I do a curry, and can manage a chicken stir fry and an excellent coq au vin. Oh yes, and bangers and mash with onion gravy. Must, must, must let your onions caramelize to get a good onion gravy!" He turned and smiled at her, picked up his glass and leaned his long frame against the cooker. "Do you like to cook?"

"I've cooked in my time, entertained, that sort of thing. I can't honestly say it's my greatest joy but I suppose I'm competent."

"Entertaining. What an appalling word that is, cast about with ritual and formality and posturing. My wife adores all that. She does business entertaining. She prefers to live in London. I prefer to live here. If you ask me, there's nothing entertaining about entertaining; showing off is more how I'd describe it. Now this," the sweep of his arm took in the entire kitchen and he smiled fondly, "this is entertaining; this place, this time, where everything has been carefully and thoughtfully chosen with joy, delight being the objective." He picked up a brass pestle and clinked it against the mortar. "The ingredients and the freshly crushed spices will combine to give you an adventure of taste." Smiling, he saluted her with his glass. "These beautiful glasses, found at a car boot, undoubtedly turn of the century when they knew about glasses. See the slenderness of the stems, the delicacy of the glass, the fineness of the subtle engraving and yet the generosity of the goblets. Perfect for my Barossa Valley Chardonnay. Wine should appeal to all five senses. You see its lovely colour. You smell its delicious bouquet." He held the glass to his nose. "You taste it on your tongue and feel it in your mouth and," he flicked the glass with his finger and listened to its clear note, "your ear too is involved." Aidan moved to the table and touched her glass with his so both chimed. "The table also will delight you."

He put down his glass and deftly arranged the cutlery and then was gone, returning with ornate silver candelabra complete with four blue candles which he placed carefully in the centre of the table. From the fridge he brought six beaten brass bowls of dips and chutneys and from the oven a pink-flowered platter with pakoras and masala varda. "Now, dip away and tell me what you think."

Alison was amused and dipped with interest.

"Delicious. Minty and spicy and a little crunchy too." She smiled at him. Aidan sat opposite her, the sleeves of his shirt pushed up past his elbows, the tail escaping from his jeans. His whole demeanour was one of relaxed anticipation and Alison was enchanted. She recollected briefly the endless embassy dinners, long shiny tables, immaculate staff, and the search for mutually agreeable conversation with total strangers. What had it all been for? Fun was certainly not part of the equation. As the evening continued, she felt more and more that she was with someone she'd known for a long time. He was right. His whole objective did seem to be to delight; not to impress or show off, but to have fun and enjoy good company and good food. His curry was rich and deeply satisfying, the rice light and fluffy. There were crisp papadums and creamy raita, crispy fried onions and hardboiled egg with raisins to accompany the curry and it was followed by simple fresh fruit salad.

Aidan told her about his family, his life, how he changed direction and now loved the opportunity to paint seriously.

"Susan can't manage the country. No gym, no take-away

cappuccino, too far from the buzz and the hype. The girls come now and then, sometimes with friends for a country weekend. But when any of them come they try to tidy me up and then it takes me days to find anything. Sometimes I have to go to London. Susan brushes me up and makes me have my hair cut and I'm polite to people and soberly dressed and occasionally I have something in one of the London galleries, but mostly I'm very happy here. Now, just a small digestif otherwise neither of us will get a wink of sleep." Again he was gone and returned with short-stemmed heavily cut crystal glasses and a sticky looking bottle. "Poire William. Not vastly alcoholic and I'll give you just a tiny bit, but I promise you'll thank me for it." He poured. "Now, tell me about you." And she did; just the facts, not the emotional depths. She didn't want to spoil the feeling of relaxed contentment.

"Aidan, I've had the most lovely evening. Thank you so much. I've loved every minute and I think your cooking is terrific."

"Thank you. I knew you'd enjoy it. That's what life's for, you know." He sat up straight and looked serious. "We have a duty to enjoy the life we're given." He relaxed. Reaching across the table and taking her hand in his he said softly, "You've had a tough time. I can see how hurt you've been, still are. But the thing is, it's no good relying on other people for our happiness. We have to find it ourselves, then we can share it. But in reality, no one is responsible for someone else's happiness."

"They can bloody well be responsible for someone else's unhappiness," Alison said bitterly.

"I know. But when you emerge from dealing with this you'll find a contentment you can't even dream of now. I'd like to be part of your contentment."

Surprised, she withdrew her hand and he let her go.

"Listen to me," he said with a light laugh, "I sound just like one of those agony aunts. Seriously though, you know I think you have great potential with your artistic ability. I really hope you'll make a go of this."

Tiredness crept over Alison. She hadn't expected to feel so bitter about James this evening and she certainly wasn't ready for any interest from Aidan. Now she felt she must at least offer to help to clear up. She stood.

"Please, let me…"

"Help with the washing up? Absolutely not. It can be done in the morning. What I want you to do is be wafted home in a haze of contentment and rest your lovely head on your pillow and sleep the sleep of the innocent. Tomorrow is a new day and one in which I have no doubt you will do your duty and enjoy whatever life brings."

Aidan saw her to her car, and held out his hand. "Keys please."

"What?"

"Keys. I shall drive you home and walk back myself. Come along. No argument." She handed him the keys.

It was just as he had said. When her head hit the pillow, she drifted into a deep and dreamless sleep. *And I didn't even say thank you properly* was her last thought.

8

I n the damp late winter days with mist clinging to dripping trees and car tyres swishing through puddles outside in the lane, Alison found herself being dragged down by life in the country. Settling in to The Stables and Highvale, the pace of her life had slowed as she became more organised. Now the projects were nearly done and this morning as she got ready for Maggie and Jake coming she realised that although she valued what was a growing sense of permanence and she could feel her roots gratefully exploring and sinking deeper into the earth of this place, of this time in her life, it puzzled her that contentment seemed elusive. She'd been down to Ed and Giselle's and joyfully shared the lives of Toby and Chloe. She'd been to London and caught up with friends, to the theatre and, with Aidan, an exhibition more than once. She knew she couldn't live her life through the lives of her children. She must respect their independence. Letting them go felt more difficult now, without James. Only when she was painting did she feel wrapped in some sense of wellbeing.

With her paper secured to her board and carefully placed at a slight angle, Alison would lightly draw her subject. She'd

shake her head and make small clicking noises. No, no, this was
not right; carefully rub out and try again. Better. Satisfied, she
would prepare the colours on her palette, not too many mixes,
don't want the colours to be muddy. She'd smile, nod, content,
yes, that looked hopeful. She loved the clink of her brushes and
the bubbling of the water as she rinsed them vigorously in her
large jam jar. Washing the paper with clear water and a large
brush she'd then begin to drop in her colour, sucking up excess
paint with a dry brush or blotting with some kitchen roll. Bent
over her board, breathing quietly, her hands deftly moved from
jar to paints to paper and back again. Occasionally she'd lean
back, squint at her work, turn her head to change the angle, get
up and walk away to look again from a distance. Her painting
was becoming a passion and she knew she was gaining in
knowledge and skill with each passing day.

Alison was becoming more established in the village, going
out for supper and inviting fellow class members to The Stables
for lunch. She was getting to know Virginia better but she was
conscious of trying not to look like 'an item' with Aidan. There
was no doubt he was a great teacher but hovering on the edge
of her contentment was a shadow, something which threatened
to dull this fragile feeling of happiness; threatened to blot it out
and return her to the misery of abandonment. No. She shook
herself. Not as bad as that. Never again would she permit
herself to be in a position where someone could hurt her as
James had done. But what was her life about? What was the
point of it? What was the point of painting pictures, even if
someone was eventually misguided enough to buy them?

The arrival of Maggie with her bags and bustle swept
Alison into the present.

"Jake's just pulled up behind me so it's all go here today."
She was into the hall, shoes changed, hoover out and heading
for the stairs. "There'd better be no mud on my clean floors,
that's all I can say, Alison. I've got my work cut out today. I

need to be off quick as you like. David's in hospital." She was up the stairs and the hoover was on.

David in hospital? Why? No time to find out, Jake was already in the courtyard. Alison shrugged herself into her gardening jacket, now battered and bulgy with pockets full of gloves and secateurs, plant ties, old glasses with the side taped up, a pencil and bits of paper.

"Hi there, Jake. Damp morning again."

"Great for planting." He handed her his Rooibos teabags. "I think we'll have cracked it by the end of the day. You coming out too?"

"Yup. I'll start you off with a mug, and then let's get going." No point in asking Maggie why David was in hospital. She probably wouldn't say anyway. Confidentiality. Funny though, Virginia hadn't said anything. But then, why would she? Virginia was involved with so many things, here one minute, away the next. That's exactly what I don't miss, Alison decided, that rushing off at the beck and call of a man, supporting his activities, running around for his projects.

"Thanks." Jake put down his spade. "So what d'you think? Nearly there?"

"I just love the feeling that everything is sitting here waiting expectantly. The trellises on the wall are devoid of greenery, but those little plants at the bases are poised to start scrambling up them. And I can see the bulbs coming up and what are those more frilly looking leaves over there?"

"That's anemone blanda. Little white ground-cover flowers. Little starry jobs ready to twinkle away on dull days."

Alison blinked. How poetic. Must be the Rooibos. "The herb garden is great. It looks more like a potager, really, like you see in those garden magazines. I've seen the green shoots of the clematis just starting too. And this beautiful little tree where I'll sit with coffee on summer mornings. What is it again?"

"Crab apple. It'll have blossom in the spring, leaves all summer, coloured leaves in the autumn and then little golden fruits in the winter. The birds will love those when there isn't much else around for them. This little tree will really earn its place in your garden."

"I hadn't appreciated there's such a seasonal rhythm in a garden. All the gardens I've had have either been tropical and without a season at all or have been professionally looked after and didn't feel like mine, even temporarily."

"Course there's a rhythm. It's nature's momentum; an ever changing thing. That's part of the joy and fascination for me." He cradled his mug and leant his skinny frame against the wall. "There's a force going on that's unstoppable but if you go with it, it's a wonderful feeling. You need to understand it; know what's possible and harness the energy. For me, gardening is creative, intellectual and sensual all at the same time." Jake dumped his mug on the wall and stretched his hands towards her, his fingers moving. "Feeling the earth with your fingers, feeling its dampness and smelling its goodness when you're planting, and knowing how the plant will flourish and give you joy as you nurture it. It's wonderful." He smiled his crooked smile into the silence which pooled between them, cocked his head on one side and briefly touched her shoulder. "You OK?"

"Yes, yes. Of course. Just feeling a bit wintry, I suppose. Wintry outside and wintry inside," she finished with a mutter.

"OK. Got to buckle down and get on with this. The seasons won't wait and wintry or not there's lots to do. Come on. Let's get going."

Jake plunged his fork into the damp soil, turning it and working it, now and then sprinkling small amounts of nourishing bone meal into it. Alison prepared the last of the plants, collecting them together and loosening them by tapping the bottom of the pots. Digging finished, Jake stood back and leant on his fork.

"OK. Now, tall ones at the back and shorter growers towards the front. We'll place them all on the soil and then stand back to see what we think."

"Well, you'll have to tell me which will be tall and which will be short."

Jake picked up a pot. "You really are a novice, aren't you? See this label? It tells you the height of the plant. Tall at the back, short at the front."

"Oh come on. That'll take me ages. I'll have to read all the labels and suss which is tall and which is short. I mean, what is tall for a plant?"

"OK. Well this one, Dicentra spectabilis, will grow up to 1.2 metres and this hosta will be 30 centimetres."

"Yes, I see that. I'm not completely stupid. But it's going to take me a lot longer than it would take you." She folded her arms and raised her chin.

Jake smiled. "I'm sorry. I don't mean to be dictatorial and after all, you're paying me to do this for you. But looking at the labels will begin to give you information, involve you with your plants. If I plant them all and you just watch them come up, your garden will merely be something you've bought, not something you care about."

"And what does that matter? Why should I care about it? Why should I care about anything? Caring just leads to sadness." Her eyes suddenly filled with tears which she defiantly brushed away with a muddy hand.

"If it was appropriate I'd give you a really good hug." He held out his arms.

Alison laughed. "Hugs are good things. Thank you for the offer. But I've got work to do."

Alison read all the labels, judged the heights, sorted the plants into groups. She read the labels for lavender and sage, iris and anchusa, viola and euphorbia, campanula and hydrangea. By the time she got to heuchera, tellima and epimidium the names she'd first read had left her head.

"Well, there you go. That's the best I can do. I have never seen a more unpromising collection of anything, but the labels are lovely, even if the names are totally incomprehensible."

Jake stood the last plant on the waiting soil. "That look OK?"

"I'll take your word for it, Jake. You know how they'll all grow."

Alison collected up the empty pots and stacked them neatly behind the shed. Her garden was nearly finished. She looked with satisfaction at the compost bins against the wall, the neat tool shed, the ornate little gazebo and the smooth flagstones, shiny and wet in fine drizzle. But her mind turned again to David. Why was he in hospital? Had there been an accident? Impatiently, she stomped her way towards the house.

"Come in and have a cup of tea before you go," she said to Jake. "I'm going in now, out of this relentless wet."

"It's a great gardening day. Look, you can almost see these little fellas squirming with delight, getting their roots into this lovely rich soil."

"Rather them than me!" Alison kicked off her boots and stuck them upside down on the boot rail, gratefully entering the dry warmth of her house, her tired feet feeling the solid flagstones under her socks. Maggie was clattering down the stairs with her hoover.

"Time for a break, Maggie?"

"Don't mind if I do but it'll have to be a quick one today."

"Why's David in hospital?" The question was out before Alison could stop herself. "No, no. Don't worry. I shouldn't have asked. I'm sure it's confidential."

"Course it is. He's been in a week and tomorrow he's coming home. That's why Kellie-Ann and me'll have to go round to his place. To get ready again." Maggie spoke as though Alison would know what this was all about, as though it was common knowledge, and yet would give Alison no details.

"I know nothing of this you know, Maggie. I've only met him, David, well properly, to talk to you know, once."

"Really?" Maggie sipped her tea. "Well, all I can say is we're all, the whole village as well as his family, hoping this is the last time. Still, there'll be a bit to do before we can be sure if it's the last time. I wouldn't be surprised if the papers'll get hold of it too. Won't hear anything from any of us, of course. Likes his privacy does David. Publicity's OK when he's working, he says, but he doesn't want to know if it's to do with his private life."

"You know, Maggie, I have always thought of myself as a polite sort of person, someone who is courteous and not nosy and not a gossip, that kind of thing. But I find myself really tempted to ask you to give me the lowdown about David. Why is publicity OK when he's working? What is his work?"

"Aha! So you're curious are you? Well I'm really surprised you don't know and if it was anyone else you were asking they'd tell you, but…"

"Really Maggie," Alison's mug hit the work surface with crash, "not the confidentiality again. Surely this is public knowledge, what a person does for a living?"

Maggie slid off her stool and took her mug to the sink, picking up Alison's on the way. "Sometimes it is and sometimes it isn't and I know what confidentiality means. It means you keep information to yourself unless your client gives you permission or is at risk. David has not given me permission."

"Well, fine. We'll leave it at that. I find I'm no longer so curious."

To HER SURPRISE, Nick came to The Stables again, this time for a few days.

"Hi Mum," he'd stood, beaming, at the front door, bag over his shoulder, his British racing green van with its Pentarron logo parked in the lane behind him. "OK if I stay a few days? Doing the historic grand prix at Jessop's Hill."

It took no more than a day for Nick's boots to be in the hall, his laptop on the dining-room table, a chair shifted in front of the television, an empty mug on the floor beside it. He came and went as he always had done, sometimes getting back long after Alison was in bed.

"You certainly work long hours, Nick."

"Yeah, well, there's a lot to do setting things up and stuff." He smiled, pushed his hands deep in his pockets and rocked back on his heels briefly. "And there's Kellie-Ann."

"Kellie-Ann?"

"She's a great girl. She's coming to Jessop's Hill with me on Saturday."

So this was the explanation for his stay in Highvale. Alison smiled. "She's certainly a live wire," she said.

"Electric," said Nick. "Anyway, I'm out of here."

He was gone and the house settled into its accustomed quiet — until, a few moments later, the phone rang. It was Virginia Rowbottom.

"Alison? Oh good. You're at home. I have a huge favour to ask you. I'm coming round at once."

SHE ARRIVED CARRYING a basket and rushed through the door and into the kitchen.

"This is such an imposition." She put the basket on the work surface. "It's David. I've had a dire call for help from Annabel and will really have to go, and these are meals for David and of course he can't yet do them himself and it's not a day Maggie or Kellie-Ann can give us any extra help, so please would you be able to fill in for me? Just 'til I can get back?"

"Virginia, will you please sit down and tell me what this is all about? Of course I'll help if I can but I haven't the faintest idea what you're talking about and I have no idea what's wrong with David."

"Really? You don't know anything?"

"Nothing."

"Well, David's recovering from further surgery for his injury and all you have to do is go over there and see he has his lunch and, if I'm not back, heat up this casserole I've got here. He'll tell you if there's anything else he needs."

"And how do you think he'll feel when he sees me? We haven't exactly hit it off, you know."

"Come now, he'll be pleased to have your help. Anyway, he has no choice. Annabel needs me. My daughter comes first and I have to go to London and if he's grumpy you can just see he's got everything and leave him to it. It'll be his own fault. This is the number for the key safe, which is behind a water butt."

"Virginia, I'm not so sure this is a good idea."

"What's not a good idea?"

"Me going to help David."

Virginia looked at her in disbelief. "Alison, this is not an idea. This is not some sort of creative endeavour. This is me with too many needs to meet asking you, as a friend, to take lunch to David. For heaven's sake, where's your problem?"

"Oh all right. But if we're being frank, and it appears we are, I think your brother-in-law is bloody rude, particularly, it seems, to me, and I'll do this for you but I might as well make it clear, now, that I do find him difficult."

"I'm not asking you to have a relationship with him, Alison. I'm asking you to heat up a casserole." Virginia yanked her car keys out of her pocket. "OK?"

Alison sighed. "You'd better tell me where he lives and what time you want me to do this."

9

Alison shut her front door firmly behind her and set off with determination. I can't believe I'm doing this, she thought. I feel like Little Red Riding Hood. I'm walking through a village carrying a basket with someone's lunch in it, someone I hardly know whose incapacity is a complete mystery to me. He's the wolf, sitting there waiting for me. All that's missing is a checked cloth in the basket. It's Cath Kidston instead.

She saw the sign, 'The Glebe' and turned off the village High Street, walking into a road of neat houses. She stopped in surprise. These houses looked as if they were built in the sixties, probably when planning permission was in its infancy. They seemed completely out of character with the rest of the village. There were no fences or hedges, just grass running down to the pavement. Number three was modern and box-like, with an in and out driveway. Its wide windows took up much of the wall space. The Trailblazer was parked in a big open car port right in front of the house. She rang the bell and then remembered Virginia's instruction about getting a key from the key safe.

"Sorry," she yodelled encouragingly through the letterbox,

"Don't worry. Getting the key." She retrieved the key from behind a water butt. This was quite ridiculous. She felt nervous. I am, she thought, right out of my comfort zone. She kicked off her wellington boots. The key slid sweetly into the lock and she was in the house, the door closed behind her. Alison stood motionless, both hands grasping her basket.

She saw a neat staircase running up the wall to her right. At the end of the hall and tucked in beside the staircase was what looked like a large open-sided cabinet with stainless-steel poles rising to the first floor. The whole of the ground floor was an open space, the wooden floor clear of rugs. There were bookshelves lining the lower wall space from the doorway round the entire room and underneath both windows. She'd never seen books arranged so beautifully neatly or at such an odd level. Above the books she was aware of huge pictures, framed photographs of skies and landscapes and flying aircraft, the glass reflecting the light. She was acutely aware of the firmness of the floor she felt beneath her socks and of the heavily book-lined lower walls. Above her the vistas of clouds and sky and distant panoramic landscapes seemed light and airy. She felt anchored at a lower level and drawn upwards by the lightness above her.

And then she saw him, a still figure at one end of a big, battered tan leather sofa, sitting peculiarly erect in spite of the comfortable curves of the sofa. He wore a black tracksuit and she could see stainless steel rods emerging from its top and meeting with a band which held his head in place. His hair was tousled, accommodating the band. His face was pale, his jaw dark with stubble. He sat silent, one arm on the arm of the sofa, the other limp across his lap. He seemed to be leaning against some bright blue fabric and sitting on something like sheepskin. He was looking at her, his face expressionless, waiting.

Alison shifted the weight of her basket to one hand and took a hesitant step forward.

"Good morning," she said, smiling. "Virginia asked me to bring you this." She held up the basket. Silence. She cleared her throat. Steely grey eyes regarded her. Why did he sit there so still and so silent? Well, this was silly. She began to feel annoyed. Even silent and motionless and clearly debilitated, this man had the power to annoy her. She moved forward, resolutely.

"Virginia has had to rush up to London for one of the girls. She asked me to bring this for you and said you would tell me what I should do." She had moved forwards and reached the space in front of him and could now see an open-plan kitchen, bright white and stainless steel, a continuation of the room she was in. There was a faint whiff of bleach, or was it the smell of hospitals? "Shall I take this into the kitchen and sort it?"

He cleared his throat. "Yeah. Sure." He watched her go into the kitchen and look around her, putting the basket on the work surface. She took off the flowery cover and peered into it.

"You're going to have to give me a hand here." She winced. He was obviously incapable of giving anyone a hand anywhere. "I mean, please tell me what you'd like me to do next. Shall I tell you what's here and then you can choose and say what you'd like me to put out for you?" She turned and looked at him. My goodness. What if he needed feeding? That would be very awkward.

"There's no need to treat me like a child. Am I to understand that you've come here with your basket, tripping round the village like Little Red Riding Hood on some errand of mercy with no information at all regarding your objective?"

Alison put a hand on the work surface to steady herself, trying to contain her irritation. "How do you do it? How do you manage to make such effortlessly rude remarks?"

"Whether what I said is rude or not is surely subjective.

Rudeness may be in the ear of the listener, not the deliverer. I asked you a simple question. Have you no information at all about your objective? This would be useful knowledge for me. I would then know I have to start at square one and give you precise instruction from the beginning. If it's just a matter of choice, then I can simply give you my decision."

"Look. I have come away from my garden to…"

"I can see that." His eyes travelled from her battered jacket to her less than pristine jeans stuffed into thick boot socks. "But you're not really Mary Mary Quite Contrary today, are you? Or perhaps you are. Quite contrary." He had raised one eyebrow and his gaze had become challenging.

"OK. Shall we get this over with?" She took the contents out of the basket. "Where is the fridge? This is your casserole for this evening which I hope devoutly someone else is going to deal with. Ah. Here." She opened the door of a large brushed steel fridge and neatly inserted Virginia's Worcester porcelain casserole. "Now, there are some sandwiches, yoghurt, some tomatoes and a flask." She undid the flask and closed it again. "Soup. Carrot, I think. There we are. Your turn now." Why did everything she said come straight out of the nursery?

"Plate in the cupboard to your left. For sandwiches. Mug above right for soup. Tomatoes in the fridge. Teaspoon for yoghurt, drawer beside the sink. Tray perfectly obvious. In front of you."

"Fine. Now, in order to be sure that I have understood my objective, when I have assembled these items, what shall I do with them?" The hand on the sofa moved and a finger pointed. The rest of his body remained motionless.

"Table." She could see a tubular framed over-bed table by the window. She could also see some sort of mechanism on the ceiling and noticed a collection of remote controls on the sofa beside him. His right hand moved and picked one up. The television came on. Well, really. He could even be rude without speaking.

Alison followed the instructions in silent exasperation, placed David's lunch on his tray and positioned the table where she thought he could reach it. He watched the news. She put the tray on the table and took the door key out of her pocket, dragging out some green string, a plant label and a tissue at the same time. Having disentangled the key she announced, "I'm going now," and headed for the door.

"Watch out for wolves on the way home."

Alison was careful to slam the door. She shoved her feet into her boots and replaced the key in its safe. And then she thought, was I a bit hasty? I didn't give him a drink of water or anything. He's stuck on that sofa and can't move. What if he needs the loo? Damn it. I'll have to find out. She stood uncertainly outside the front door. The voices on the television stopped. She heard music. Well, he had all those remotes to hand, he must have a phone too. He'd be able to call someone. And yet how thoughtless not to give him a drink. She got the key out again, opened the letterbox, bent down and called, "I forgot something. Coming back in."

Standing in the hall in her boots, she saw David had a bottle of water in his hand. "Ah. That was what I was coming back for. I felt I should have given you a drink with your lunch."

"Ah," he echoed, "I'd have included it with my instructions. Have a supply beside me."

"Look. This is not some kind of contest. If I'm asked to do something I do it properly, so I don't really care if I unwittingly offer you another opportunity to be rude to me because I'm going back to my garden as soon as I leave here and there's nothing more soothing than plants, I can tell you, so…"

"My rudeness, as you call it, causes you to need soothing, does it?"

"No. In fact it doesn't. But I'm going to finish this now. Have I done everything I can for you?" How else could she put it?

"Well that depends on what you have in mind." His words and his slow drawl sounded incongruous coming from a man with such a rigid formal posture, but did she see a light in his eyes and was he almost smiling?

"I had in mind the loo," she managed.

"Oh." He raised his eyebrows in exaggerated surprise. "And how did you imagine you would help me with that?"

Bother. This was a big mistake. She should have just left. "Look. Can't you just put down this stupid attitude of yours? Do you or do you not need help with the loo? I imagined you might have some sort of bottle thing to pee into like they do in hospitals and it would need emptying, which I would do, and then you'd be fine until whoever comes to you next, came. I know nothing at all about your present situation, since everyone who does is bound to some sort of silence…"

"So you've enquired, have you?"

Alison ignored his remark and his interruption. "Do you or do you not need any more help?"

"I do not need any more help."

"Goodbye."

"Goodbye."

This time she shut the door with the utmost quietness, replaced the key and left.

THERE WAS quiet stillness in The Stables when she got home. The house smelt of furniture polish and there was a pleasant feeling of orderliness from Maggie's last visit. Even the coats in the hall looked neatly arranged. Everything was beautifully controlled and she knew this was her comfort zone. Alison hung up her jacket and extracted her feet from her boots.

Well, at least she'd got her domestic arrangements nicely sorted and now she'd check out the garden again. Her visit to The Glebe had rattled her. Each encounter with David Rowbottom left her feeling unsure of herself, somehow, and took the shine out of life. How could a person you hardly knew have this effect? It was enormously irritating. She had met some deeply boring people in her time, had to be charming to them, to sublimate her personal feelings and managed with no problem. But this was different. Every encounter with David was completely unproductive and there was no reason for her to spend any time with him at all. So she wouldn't. That was a definite.

The weather had cleared and the small garden looked immaculate. Jake had swept the flagstones and the whole court-yard had an air of expectancy. Spring would come and things would happen. Alison found herself sharing the feeling that something would happen. But what? What might happen? Oh the bulbs would come up all right and the blossom would flower but what was going to happen in her life? What would she be doing? Her optimism evaporated. What indeed? Well, she thought, one thing was for sure. Whatever it was it was up to her to do it herself. No one was going to do it for her. She'd learned that much at least.

As she came in from the garden, the phone rang.

"Virginia? Hi. Yes, all was well and in spite of his appalling attitude and his apparent charm by-pass I think you could say the objective was met." She paused, pleased with her efforts until she heard Virginia with breathless apology ask if she could go back to David's in the evening.

"Maggie went this afternoon and she'll tuck David up later but please could you be an angel and sort the supper? I'm just not going to get back in time. Seven o'clock, OK?"

There was silence. "Alison? You there?"

"I'm here. I don't really have a choice, do I?"

"Oh thank you, thank you. I owe you. I'm truly grateful." Alison heard a click and Virginia was gone.

DUSK WAS GATHERING when Alison went upstairs to get out of her gardening clothes. She pulled on soft grey wool trousers which tapered to the ankle, a fine, ivory cotton knit top and a stylish acid green chunky cardigan and slipped on a pair of black suede pumps. Looking critically at herself in the mirror, she applied minimal moisturiser and makeup, highlighting her cheeks with a peachy glow and finishing with the lightest spray of fragrance. She brushed her hair and then ran her fingers through it before clipping it loosely back. She regarded herself in the mirror. Did I really do that? Did I really take all that trouble just because I'm going to put a casserole in an oven? Well maybe it's because I need some sort of armour, to defend myself. She recognised the defiance in her reflection and shook herself, turning determinedly away from the mirror and going downstairs. It was only six o'clock. She slumped into a chair and put on the news.

Images of vast arid landscape and dust raised by vehicles crossed the screen and changed to views of tented camps, hungry people and whimpering children. The voice of the commentator was energetic. The war was apparently over. These people could look forward to a peace brought about by the men in blue helmets, but their infrastructure had been destroyed and many children would call these camps home for a long time to come. Alison looked about her, grateful for her cosy security. The front door opened and in walked her robust, well-fed son, the embodiment of youthful potential thanks to his fine education and the opportunities he'd been fortunate enough to encounter. She turned down the television.

"Hi Mum!" Nick threw himself onto the sofa. "What a day. Good to be back."

"I have to go out briefly at about seven. Are you in this evening?"

"I'll just get myself a sandwich if that's OK and I'll be out for a bit myself. I'll have a quick shower first." He was up and off, grabbed an apple from the fruit bowl as he passed it and clattered up the stairs. Life is plentiful for you, my son, thought Alison, but for many it isn't. She looked at her watch. Six forty-five. Should she go now? Was the casserole to be ready at seven or was she to arrive at seven? Oh good grief, she'd have to stay until the damn thing was heated through. Well stuff this, she thought as apprehension began to creep over her, I shall go now anyway. What am I doing sitting here like some schoolgirl waiting for an exam? She stood in the hall contemplating her jacket options, thinking this too was ridiculous. Now she couldn't make a decision of which jacket to wear! She opened the door. Was it raining? Was it windy? No, but it was getting dark and quite cold. She'd take the car and wear her old gardening jacket. No need to dress up for someone to be rude to her.

As SHE DROVE the short distance to The Glebe her apprehension subsided and she found herself thinking sympathetically about David and his situation. Why was she only thinking of herself? The poor guy had problems she was lucky not to have. I'll do what Virginia said, she decided. I'll just get on with it. Before she opened the door, Alison yoo-hooed through the letterbox again.

"Helloohoo. You'll be overjoyed to know it's little Red Riding Hood back again," and she was in the hall discarding her jacket and walking purposefully into David's living room. He looked at her with dull eyes and didn't move. She stopped and her heart skipped a beat. Poor guy, he looked so dejected and somehow hopeless.

"Hello," she smiled, "I hope it's not my arrival that's made you so gloomy."

He sighed deeply and she watched as he made an effort to reply. "How could a little ray of sunshine in a bright green woolly make a person gloomy? No, it's not exactly your arrival…that is, it's not because it's you who've arrived. The fact that someone has to arrive at all is hardly a cause for delight, whoever it is."

"I'm sorry. I don't know what to say." Alison was completely unnerved and stood before him helplessly as his gaze held hers. A clock struck seven. "Oh. Seven o'clock. My objective beckons." She went to the kitchen and turned on the oven, extracting the casserole from the fridge, carefully avoiding looking at David.

"Virginia usually puts the oven on one eighty."

"OK. One eighty it is. Now, tell me what happens next. Do you usually have a beer or something or do you need a…"

"No, you don't have to help me to have a pee or anything. Maggie's been and she'll come again."

"Well that's OK then. So, while this is getting warm, it's the same as lunchtime, is it? The tray etcetera?"

"What a calm and patient person you're trying to be. Do you know, I can actually see you making yourself be patient and talk calmly. Do you have children? I bet that's just how you dealt with your children."

"Look David," she sat down opposite him, "I really feel for you with your present difficulties…"

"There's no need," he interrupted. "Sympathy is the last thing I need."

"Oh for heaven's sake," Alison stood up, exasperated and crushed by his immediate rejection of her friendly overture. "I'll just get your supper, shall I, and then I'll be out of your hair."

"As you wish." He turned on the television.

"Oh, I wish all right." She returned to the kitchen.

Meticulously, she drew a tray from the tray space and placed it on the work surface. Opening the cutlery drawer she extracted knife, fork and spoon and placed them neatly on the tray. She was acutely aware that he was watching every move she made. From the fridge she took strawberries, hulled them and placed them in a small bowl which went onto the tray. Refusing to look in his direction she put a plate into the oven to warm and then removed it, replacing it with a large soup bowl. She checked the casserole and closed the oven door for a few more minutes. Then she turned away from David and leant on the work surface, gazing into the gathering gloom of the garden.

All the while, David didn't move. The gloom of the evening seemed to creep into the house. She turned in David's direction. He was watching the television. As she glanced about her she realised how many hard edges and surfaces there were in this space he called home: the big square windows; hard floor; metallic-finished, huge glass-framed pictures. Where was softness, cosiness? There wasn't any. Even the books were so neat they seemed almost to stand to attention. The pale wash of colour of the books was overpowered by the monochrome, blacks, whites, greys, polished metal, of everything else. Only the huge leather sofa had any curves or contours and at least it was a warm tan colour. She found herself standing straighter, hands by her sides and then she almost laughed when she realised how bright and out of place her jacket seemed in this environment devoid of colour. Time to present the casserole.

"Thank you," said David as Alison put the tray and the fragrant casserole in its easily manageable bowl in front of him.

"So pleased to be of help. If that is all you need I'll be off. I'm going to leave my number here for you just in case."

"In case of what?"

"Well, in case you need me."

"Whatever would I need you for?"

"You will be stunned to know that since I've been here this evening I find myself completely impervious to your lack of courtesy. No, I'll rephrase that. To your rudeness. I have no idea why you're so consistently unpleasant, but I find myself unwilling to compromise my personal standards which a descent to your level of discourtesy would most certainly do. When I close your front door I will know that I've done everything I can for you and I will have done it on behalf of your sister-in-law who has been kindness itself to me ever since I arrived here. You are not the only one who has found life difficult and a little grace under pressure might make you feel better about yourself and could certainly help those around you who are trying to do their best for you."

"Grace under pressure? What the hell are you talking about?" David's eyes blazed over the steaming supper in front of him. "I freely acknowledge I'm no saint, Madam, but I suggest you confine your smart remarks to things you know a bit about. You have absolutely no idea what pressures I face. So as you are, I devoutly hope, leaving now, Madam, I bid you a graceful thank you and a graceful goodbye."

The silence as they glared at one another lengthened. Neither moved.

Alison stood, rigid, regarding the seated man, his face pale, lips grim, eyes narrowed with irritation. She sensed his latent power and felt the shock of the almost tangible energy of his frustration. His strong hands were clenched on each side of the invalid's over-bed table. Deliberately she turned her back on David and left, closing the door very quietly behind her. Damn, damn, damn, she thought. She replaced the key in the safe and got into her car. For a moment she sat clutching the steering wheel and trying to settle the turmoil within her − then, realising that without the noise of the engine he'd know she hadn't left, she started the car and drove away, not permitting herself to release the anger she felt until she reached home. The door banged shut behind her and the jacket she threw at the coat peg crumpled onto the floor. She left it there defiantly. You try to be helpful, she thought. You try to be sympathetic. You endeavour to put yourself in someone else's place and, yes, not to put too fine a point on it, bring them comfort, and all you get in return is rudeness. I just hope Virginia doesn't ask me to do that again.

I n the dark hours of early morning, Alison woke with toothache. Waiting for the painkillers to work and watching the shape of her bedroom window appear as light increased, the image of David came to her unbidden. She turned her pillow over, punched it with her fist, smoothed it and tried to settle her head, to the right and then to the left. She wriggled her shoulders and drew the duvet under her chin. Reluctantly she relived last night's confrontation. Am I a real wimp, she thought, to have reacted so furiously to the childish behaviour of this spoilt man who has no one else to think about but himself? And anyway, what does it matter? To hell with the whole business. I suppose a therapist would say I overreacted because of my own rejection. James rejected me and so has David Rowbottom. Rubbish! She sat up, legs out of bed, feet on the floor. What rubbish. What am I thinking? I did a favour for Virginia. End of story.

By mid-morning the pain was worse and her face had begun to swell. Her head throbbed and her ear seemed to be involved. With the phone to her good ear, she started phoning dentists until she found a slot for an emergency appointment.

Driving with the pain was no joke and parking was a night-mare. She looked balefully at the receptionist.

"Alison Henderson. I have an appointment."

"Ah yes. Here we are." The receptionist rested her long shiny magenta fingernail on the page in front her, smiled a glossy smile and batted sooty eyelashes. Her short bright hair was gelled and spiked and dusted with something blue. She leaned confidentially forwards, her tiny white uniform barely containing her bosom as she took a long intake of breath. "You're ever so lucky. Dick Lavender can fit you in." She closed her glossy smiling mouth and waited for Alison's response.

"Oh. Thank you. Well, I just need help with this as soon as possible."

"Ooh I can see. Poor you. You've got a swollen face there, haven't you? Come and sit down over here." She emerged from behind her reception desk, guided Alison to a seat and sat down beside her. "There, that's more comfy isn't it?"

"Thank you. Yes." Alison smiled

"You don't know Dick Lavender, do you? You're his last appointment, see, before he goes to Malawi tomorrow." Alison tried not to be irritated by this well-meaning young woman. Oh good grief spare me, she thought. I don't need a life history, I just need dental attention. But she smiled a polite smile and the receptionist enthusiastically continued. "Yes, he's taking a team with him on a teaching trip. They're all dentists or dental nurses and they're all volunteers, you know. He goes out three times a year and they teach the locals to do dental stuff. Must be ever such a relief for loads of people what never had dentists before, don't you think?" She smiled with proprietary pride.

Alison nodded. "Oh yes. Feeling the way I do I'm grateful I'm not having to walk miles through the bush to some inade-quate facility where no doubt the only option is extraction with a risk of blood poisoning."

"Oh so you know Malawi, do you?"

"Well not exactly Malawi, but I've lived in Africa and I'm familiar with Third-World situations." The receptionist patted her spiky hair and adjusted her tiny uniform as she stood up. "I expect he'll see you in a minute." She returned to her station. "Ah, there you are." With a glint of magenta, she indicated an opening door

"Alison Henderson? Please come this way. Mr Lavender will see you now."

SKILLED LATEX-CLAD fingers gently probed her open mouth and a quiet voice gave instructions to the nurse. Alison lay still in the dentist's chair, holding onto its arms but trying to relax, feeling relieved that she felt confidence in this complete stranger. Tomorrow he'd be on his way to Africa; soon, no doubt, walking into the bush with his team and making the most enormous difference to the people he encountered.

"You can rinse now, Mrs Henderson." Dick Lavender snapped off his gloves and explained her treatment. "So please make an appointment to coincide with the completion of the antibiotics and all should be well. Here are your prescriptions and remember, if you have any problems at all, get in touch and one of my partners will see you."

"Thank you so much for seeing me. I can't tell you how grateful I am. And I do hope all goes well in Malawi." He looked surprised. "Your receptionist was telling me. I think she was trying to take my mind off the pain."

"I see. Well, we're all approaching retirement and it seemed a useful thing to do now that we have more time and before we get too decrepit."

AS SHE DROVE HOME, Alison thought about the team of dentists and what she was doing with her own time and found her familiar demons keeping her company again. So what skill could I share, she thought, before I become decrepit? Let's see. I know how to hire and fire a cook; how to chat at diplomatic functions; how to write a charming thank-you note; how to pack up a house, move and resettle an entire family and I suppose you could say I have a modicum of child-rearing skill but you could hardly say those are skills required for survival or the relief of real suffering. But at least I'm pain-free, she thought.

She remembered a Christmas story Ed and Nick had loved, about a philosophical little forest tree desperate to find his purpose in life. Strange that should come into my head, she thought. Is that what I'm doing, looking for a purpose? She stopped her car outside The Stables. Well, the little tree might have been thrilled to have been cut from the forest to be a Christmas tree, but I'm happy where I am. And here is where I'll be staying, so there'd better be a purpose here.

A FEW DAYS later Aidan arrived at The Stables, multi-coloured stripy scarf wrapped several times round his neck and a large battered old canvas bag under his arm.

"Oh, it's good to see you, Aidan."

"You do seem really pleased to see me."

"I am. To be honest, I've felt a little low. Had a dental problem." She put a hand to her cheek. "I'll put the kettle on. Go through and I'll join you."

Aidan stretched his long legs towards the fire and settled appreciatively into the comfortable chair.

"A mug would have done," he said as Alison put down a pretty tray and began to pour tea into china cups.

"Oh no it wouldn't. This is afternoon tea. Have a biscuit."

"So how are things?"

"Well, OK really. Nick's still here. It seems he's quite centrally placed here, even though he's sometimes away a couple of nights or so, and it's convenient for him to pick up his mail here and of course," she leaned forward smiling, "there's Kellie-Ann."

"Who's Kellie-Ann?"

"Maggie's daughter. Maggie and Tony Scutter."

"Oh. Right."

"Nick was smitten by Kellie-Ann the minute he saw her so I think she's probably the biggest reason why he's still here. I like his company and she's a complete bundle of energy and really good for him."

"And what about you? How are you? Ready for another of my curries or a trip to a gallery in London?"

"Oh I'm much better now this dental thing is settling. You're sweet to take an interest."

"I'd take much more of an interest if you'd let me." He looked at her steadily, his face composed and serious.

"Oh Aidan. Please be my friend. You know how things are for me. I'm not looking for a relationship. I'm just trying to get my feet firmly on the ground. My entire world was wrecked when James left me, not only my present world but my future world too. It was as though he'd torn up everything that I valued, believed in, everything that was me and thrown the pieces in my face. I don't know if I will ever be able to bring myself to rely on anyone else again, you know, to be able to completely share and to allow myself to be vulnerable."

"You must have given this a lot of thought. You seem to have it all worked out." Aidan's voice was soft.

"Of course I've thought about it. I've had these horrendous feelings of rejection, felt lost and alone, panicky about the future, all the awful emotions which go with abandonment. It's been a grieving; a grieving for the togetherness with James, a grieving for my lost youth, a grieving for opportunities I won't ever have, lots of things. And then here, at The Stables which I so fell in love with, I've started to find some security, some reason for being, if you like. Oh I know it'll probably sound awfully domestic to you, but it's really mattered to me, getting the house sorted and how I like it; learning about the garden. I'm such a novice with the garden but Jake's been fantastic."

"Jake?"

"Yes. He has a gardening company. Calls himself a retread. As in tyres. This is a new career for him and he's done my tiny courtyard beautifully. It's been really good, and I know how trite this sounds, but getting back to nature has been wonderfully therapeutic. Well, not back to nature because I was always a true townie, to be honest, an international urbanite. Getting involved with seasonal things has been so soothing. Mother Nature. We all need a mother when times are hard, don't we? I'm waiting for spring now. I know where the snowdrops will come up and which is the winter flowering jasmine and I can't wait for my Sarcococca to flower. Christmas box, it's called, and the tiny flowers apparently smell wonderful. They have to, you see, because there aren't many passing insects for fertilisation in the winter, so the scent has to travel a long way." She stopped and saw that Aidan was quietly watching her. It was getting dark and the last of the cold winter light was dwindling.

"How lovely you are when you're alight with enthusiasm."

Alison felt herself flush. "I'd better put on some lights."

"Don't worry," Aidan drawled, "I got your message loud and clear and I am, believe me, your friend. Your good friend. You can trust that. So everything's tickety boo, is it, and Mother Nature's got you on an even keel, if I can mix my metaphors."

"Well I don't know. It's a strange thing, isn't it, how you can feel you're fine and then suddenly something happens and you're back to square one again with all the old doubts and uncertainties."

"Meaning what?"

"Oh I don't want to bang on about me. Men hate to talk about feelings." Alison moved about the room turning on lamps.

"I'm not talking. I'm listening. Listening is what good friends do."

"Virginia asked me to do her a favour a few days ago, and I did and I wish I hadn't." She was surprised that she'd given in to the impulse to tell him, surprised at her own vehemence. She sat down again.

"Why? What was the favour and why do you regret agreeing to do it?"

"Well," Alison shifted in her chair, fiddled with her bracelet, pushed her hair off her face.

"Go on," encouraged Aidan.

"Well, I had to go to David's house a couple of times. You know he's recovering from surgery?"

"I take it you mean David Rowbottom."

"Yes. And to be honest I was really reluctant to go because he's such an objectionable person and so damned rude. I don't need that, you know? I mean, why should anyone put up with it? Anyway, Virginia was under pressure and had to rush off for one of the girls and the carers had got tied up somewhere and it seemed a simple thing to do and Virginia got a bit exasperated with my reluctance so I agreed. She's been a great friend to me and endlessly encouraging and supportive. Anyway, I had to go to David's house twice, once at lunchtime and then in the evening and frankly he was bloody rude and I was absolutely furious," she took a deep breath and subsided back in her chair limply, "and then I thought I'd really overreacted and now I feel a complete wimp. That was the day before the tooth infection." She brightened. "Maybe that was it! I was sickening for a tooth infection."

Aidan laughed. "I don't know what you're worrying about.

You did what was asked of you. I can't see what the problem is. As you said, you did a favour for a friend and that's the bottom line."

"Thank you for that, and thank you to you for being my friend. It is lovely to feel someone values you. Helps the self-esteem no end. I did try to be sympathetic but he continually put me down. To be honest, I feel really bad that I couldn't help the poor man without annoying him."

"Poor man!" Aidan exploded. "Spoilt prima donna! My God, the guy has everything!"

"How can you say that when he's so disabled and has to use a wheelchair?"

"Don't you know his story?"

"No, I don't. I know nothing about him."

"He's an RAF fighter pilot… or was. I don't know the details. He's a bit stand-offish, to be honest. Well he is with me, anyway. They say he ejected from his plane not once, but twice, which is apparently very rare, and has been grounded while they sort him out. And what does he do while he's grounded?" Aidan was out of his chair, walking up and down and gesticulating, "he writes books. Not just any books but bestsellers, the jammy bugger. Calls himself Hal Davidson. You see his books at any airport. Must have made a fortune. I wouldn't waste any sympathy on him. You can bet he's feathered his nest very adequately."

Alison said nothing. How complicated this all seemed.

"Well," she waved her hand dismissively, "thank you for telling me but it doesn't change anything. I won't be going to The Glebe again so it's all academic really."

Aidan was standing in front of the fireplace, his hands deep in the pockets of his faded cord trousers, shoulders hunched, towering over Alison's chair. She looked at him inquiringly.

"So." He drew out his hands and headed for his old canvas bag. "This is the reason I came to see you. Now that you're so beautifully organised," he waved his arm vaguely towards the garden and round the room, "I wonder whether you're up for a new project." Aidan pulled a notebook with a battered cover from his bag and fished a pen from his pocket. He sat down, poised over the notebook. Alison waited.

"Go on."

"Well, might you have more time now?"

"I might. It might depend on what the project is."

"Art, my dear. Painting, drawing. You were talking of Mother Nature. A quote for you. 'By viewing nature, nature's handmaid, art, makes mighty things from small beginnings grow...' Dryden wrote that. And furthermore," he struck a declaiming pose, "'It is art that makes life, makes importance and I know of no substitute whatever for the force and beauty of its process.' Henry James."

Alison blinked. "Really. And the relevance of these erudite quotes, apart, of course, from demonstrating your excellent education?"

"No, no. Not so much my education as my interest in art. Now, I think the time has come to have an exhibition, open to the whole class. My class. The one you attend. What d'you think?"

"Well, what are you expecting of me?"

"Enthusiasm would be a nice start, and, as one of my star pupils, some exhibits from you as well. I'd put in a couple too, of course, but really I'd like to showcase you all and I'm quite sure some sales would be made. We'd pick the time carefully, over a weekend, you know, and do some advertising. But it would be fun, don't you think?"

Alison was silent.

"Everyone would have to start working towards it now, of course, and I will be the final judge of what we hang and where we hang it. But it's great to have something to work towards and to have a wider opinion of your work. Otherwise you're just painting for yourself."

"Well I don't see it that way. I see myself as a student, a learner. I measure my progress by comparing what I can do now with what I could do three months ago."

"Well OK, I suppose that's valid in a way. But it's hardly purposeful, is it? I mean, where's the real objective in that?"

Alison felt rattled. The little forest tree looking for its purpose crept back into her mind and she remembered the last time she was required to have an objective, a purpose, was the sorting of David's supper.

"Let's leave purpose and objective out of this, shall we? What are you really asking of me?"

"I'm honestly asking you if you'll enter into the spirit of things and work towards exhibiting your paintings. I believe you have a real talent and just turning up on a Thursday and doing your homework during the week isn't giving you the drive you need. If you were starving in a garret it would be different. But you're not, are you? You are really well provided for and don't need to earn money by painting."

"But painting for money is entirely different from painting for the joy of it."

"Where's your spirit of adventure? Break out a bit. Try something new. Explore your talent, your ability."

There was a hush. Neither spoke. Alison sat quite still, her hands resting on the arms of her chair, poised, as though she was about to move.

"Aidan," her voice was quiet and she looked intently at him, "you implied the paintings would be offered for sale, so this is clearly a commercial enterprise is it?"

"Well yes, to a degree, I suppose. I mean, not necessarily profit making. At least, that's not the reason for doing it."

"Well," Alison was out of her chair and pacing in front of the fire. "Let's make it a reason. You'll have to hire the hall and presumably either the exhibitors will pay a small fee or the cost will come out of their profits, or both. And maybe there'll be an entry fee?"

"I hadn't thought about the details yet."

"Well, what about doing it for charity? I'll help you if we can contribute to charity and I will name the charity. We'll give the whole thing a great deal of hype, definitely charge an entry fee to viewers, raffle a painting, have a gala opening with a celebrity, everything. What do you think?"

"Well, what a transformation. I can't believe it. Look at you, practically bursting with enthusiasm. Are you saying not only will you put some paintings in, you'll also help to organize the event?"

"I am indeed. A light has dawned. I love the idea and I love the challenge and maybe, just maybe, I have found a purpose. You see Aidan, I can't go to Malawi and teach people dental skills and people who are really up against it don't need to hire or fire a cook. Do they? You're quite right to look confused, my friend. I have a bottle of something modest but delicious in my fridge and we will share it now. You'll find glasses in that cupboard over there. Dwell in possibility, Aidan. I have no idea who said it, but it's on a magnet on my fridge door so someone must have done. And that's what I'm going to do. After we've shared the wine, of course."

11

"Maggie, I've been thinking about it. I don't think you have to worry about it anymore."

"You what?" Maggie stashed the hoover into its place under the stairs and eased herself onto a kitchen stool. "I'm ready for this coffee, I can tell you. What a rush this morning. I didn't leave David's 'til half nine. What don't I have to worry about anymore?"

"Confidentiality."

"You've lost me. What are you talking about?"

"David Rowbottom. I've been part of the team. I've been to his house and I know about the surgery. Virginia asked me to help."

"I know. Went all right did it, your time at The Glebe?" Alison's eyes narrowed as she looked at Maggie.

"I suspect you know exactly how it went, Maggie. Did David not fill you in?"

"Sometimes David talks a lot and sometimes he don't say nothing."

"I see. Well what I was saying was, now that I've been

involved don't you think this confidentiality stuff needn't apply anymore?"

"I don't see the difference, Alison. I mean, I take things serious, I do. I don't talk about clients I'm giving care to and I wouldn't talk about you neither. What is it you want to know?"

"Why should I want to know anything?"

"I don't know. It was you brought it up, not me." Maggie looked inscrutable.

"If I'm honest, Maggie, and I would want you to keep this confidential please, I just don't understand why he's so grumpy and difficult and downright rude. How can you have patience with people like that? I mean, yes it's tough for him, being disabled and in a wheelchair, but that doesn't give him carte blanche to behave just as he feels like with whoever comes his way, even to help him. Does it?"

"Ain't never been rude to me." Maggie smiled. "Been rude to you, has he?"

"All the time," Alison blurted out. "Not that I've seen much of him, really, but every time I do I can't seem to say a single thing that's right and in fact most of what I say seems to be wrong."

"And you mind, right? You care about what he thinks of you."

"Absolutely not. Why should I give a damn about what he thinks of me?"

"Well that's all right, then. Doesn't matter, does it? So then, this confidentiality you was on about. What is it you want to know?"

"Nothing. Forget it." Alison reached for Maggie's mug. "Finished?"

"Oh yes." Maggie smiled broadly at her. "I've finished. But I don't think you have." She patted Alison affectionately on the shoulder. "So nice to see my Kellie-Ann and your Nick so happy, don't you think? She talks about him all the time, she does. And he's such a nice boy. Works hard too, doesn't he? Well, I'll be on my way. See you next Tuesday. Unless I see you at The Glebe before that, of course."

"I think that's very unlikely, Maggie."

It was cold in the garden but sheltered where Alison had set up her easel. She sat quietly on her stool, taking in her surroundings. Aidan had repeated frequently that it was worth spending time looking at what you want to paint, noticing how the light fell and thinking about the colours. She'd have to use browns and greens and lovely purple and grey shaded colours. She was determined that her attempts at painting should communicate what she felt about what she was looking at, not be merely decorative. She turned up the collar of her jacket and wriggled her toes in the thick socks that filled her boots. She saw the old wall, the brave new shoots of climbers which sought to grasp it. She saw the spears of snowdrops thrusting through the earth and the tiny waxy white flowers of Christmas box suspended under shapely glossy green leaves. Their scent clung to the shrub, waiting to be wafted on a passing breeze. What if a bee didn't pollinate? What if the climber wasn't strong enough to cling? What if late snow covered the snowdrops? There was threat. But there was hope, too. Alison grasped her pencil and began to draw.

"Alison. Hello. Are you there?" It was Virginia calling over the wall. Alison put down her pencil and let her in.

"I saw your car and knew you were in but you didn't answer the door. Oh, well done. You're painting. I've just been talking to Aidan. Such a good idea, this exhibition, don't you think? I just hope we'll be able to produce something good enough. Well, you will, I'm sure. We'll see whether I will." She peered at Alison's easel. "Hmmm. This looks a little different, for you. Normally you're so precise."

"I know. It's the map-drawing training. But I wanted to do something looser, something more meaningful. Not just an exact replication of the subject."

"My goodness, that all sounds very profound."

"Virginia, it's the strangest thing, but suddenly, since Aidan was here with his exhibition idea, I can see the possibility for a real purpose in my life."

"Can you indeed? So this is the effect Aidan has had on you, is it?"

"No, no. Not Aidan, his idea."

"But you do see quite a bit of him, don't you? And he is the most remarkably attractive man. And so nice, too. I know he thinks a lot of you."

"And how do you know that, Virginia?"

"The way he looks at you. The way his voice softens when he talks about you. The way he leans over you when he's helping you, as though he can't get close enough to you. The way you two spend so much time together."

"I am amazed that you could let such romantic nonsense enter your head, Virginia. Really. You're such a down-to-earth practical person, too. Aidan is married, for goodness' sake. He is a friend. I think of him as a friend."

"If you say so."

"I do."

"Well, you and your friend have a lot of work ahead of you and I've said I'll come on board too. The Highvale Painters will put on a really good show. First meeting, my house, next Wednesday, six thirty. OK?"

"I'll be there."

It was a noisy group in the kitchen at Highvale House. Alison loved the warmth and the friendliness and the feeling of belonging. Unwilling to encourage any ideas that she may feel linked to Aidan, she carefully sat at the far end of the table from him. Quietly she took in the group. These were the sparrows she'd watched in the pub all those months ago, fluttering and settling and chirruping joyfully. Now they were her friends, people she knew; Janet, with her crisp short hair and vast supply of pretty dangling earrings and Henry, quiet and studious who always painted heavily with acrylic. And Claudette, histrionic and chaotic with multi-coloured and multi-layered clothing and her great friend Anne, always soberly clad and who painted with remarkable detail. All were so individual, joyfully sharing the same pursuit. She looked at them in turn and met Aidan's gaze. He winked and raised an eyebrow. She flushed and sipped her wine, hoping no one had seen.

"Order, order," Aidan clapped his hands and the meeting took off. "We all know one another well and I was hoping we could do this in an informal way, without the need for minutes. I will make it clear right from the start that my decision about what we accept for exhibition is final, as we as a group are putting our reputation, if you like, into the public arena, and I trust you'll be guided by me with regard to the prices you think your work might reasonably achieve. But let's start with some discussion."

Dates, times, costs, publicity were discussed, dismissed, repeated until at last some form began to appear. Aidan took over again.

"Alison had the idea that we should find a way to include a charitable contribution. Could we have the feelings of the meeting about this please?"

Quickly, Alison took the floor. "I hope you don't mind if I say something first. It's just that we're so fortunate here, living in safety, with enough to eat and having the freedom to vote and all the things that go with life in a Western democracy. I know we all have the troubles and difficulties that life throws at us from time to time, but these days the difficulties of so many come right into our living rooms on the news, which somehow makes their tragedies so immediate and often so enduring. I wondered whether we, through the art which we so enjoy, might make a difference to the lives of people less fortunate than we are. I hope this doesn't sound horribly worthy but for me, personally, it would mean a lot if I could use my learning and whatever skill I might acquire in a really useful way. I'm prepared to put in time and effort to help with the organisation of this because in my view this is more than just a charitable contribution. I hope you won't mind me saying, Aidan, that I do think minutes are necessary because when money is involved you really have to keep everything in good order."

She sat down. Instantly there was a babble of talk as, inevitably, everyone wanted to have their say.

"We should only give to a large reliable organisation. We don't want funds going astray or spent on administration. They should go right to the people who need them."

"Why do we have to support something abroad? What about charities in this country? I mean, there are people in need right here. Look at David Rowbottom, for instance. I don't mean David himself, of course, but people like him. Other heroes whose lives have been changed forever when doing their duty."

"Well, I think it should be children. I don't care where in the world they are, as long as it's children."

"I think it shouldn't be connected with any religion or government agency. It's religion and politics which are at the root of all the world's problems."

"Order, order." Aidan stood up to speak. "Whichever organisation we choose, I think we'd better now do the formal stuff and vote. All in favour of making this a big charity event?"

Hands were raised.

"That seems unanimous. Now, who might take the minutes?" He glanced round the table.

"I'll happily do that," said Janet.

"Thank you. Now all we need, Alison, is a charity. Unless you already have an idea, perhaps you'd bring some to the next meeting."

"I will. But I'm going to say straightaway that charity these days is an industry and there's limitless choice. I have seen much charity work going on overseas and I do think to be properly supportive and to be committed you have to have a passion for what you're doing and you have to care. This can't just be lip service; we send a cheque for so much and feel good about it. Not for me, anyway. For me I have to care and I'd like to be involved with simple practicalities which make a difference to peoples' lives; things like mosquito nets or clean water. I apologise for sounding so personal but, well, I'm feeling this personally. And I hope at the next meeting I can give you details and you will feel personally too."

She sat down, amazed that she'd revealed so much of herself and smiled bravely at her fellow painters who all looked at her solemnly. Aidan was tapping the table thoughtfully. At last, he spoke.

"Well, thank you Alison. Very moving. However, please let us not lose sight of the fact that this exhibition is about you, about us, and one of its objectives is for all of us to work towards a higher personal standard and to explore our own creativity. See you all at the next class."

ALISON WAS SLIPPING on her coat and feeling in her pocket for her torch when Aidan joined her.

"Mind if I walk you home? I've parked outside the back of The Stables."

"Have you? Why did you do that?"

"It seemed convenient."

"Not as convenient as parking in the drive of Highvale House, surely."

"Well, perhaps there was an ulterior motive."

"Let's walk." They left by the back door and headed down the driveway. Alison shone the torch and kept her distance.

"Do you think that went OK?" he asked.

"Yes. Fine. Why do you ask?"

"I didn't want you to feel I was in opposition at all; that I wasn't entirely happy about this link with a charity."

"Are you happy about it?"

"I'm happy to have you on board and helping me with this but I don't want to lose sight of the fact that the main reason for doing this is the painting."

"Aidan, I don't see what the problem is. You want an exhibition, I'm sure for your own paintings too and you want to encourage us. That will happen. Whether we make a bit of money for charity or not doesn't change that."

"Well, it does if the thrust of any publicity is about the charity. I saw a new you in there this evening. I can tell you've either done this sort of thing before, or if you haven't you'll be very good at it."

"Of course I've been involved in stuff like this, Aidan, I was married to a diplomat and spent years abroad in a representational role. I can do this. But I value these friends, and you, and this class, all part of Highvale and my healing process, if you like, and I wouldn't dream of jeopardising any of that. That's why it's good to have meetings and minutes and listen to opinion and act in agreement with everyone. Aren't you being a bit of a purist thinking of doing this with an 'art for art's sake' mentality? Surely the important thing is to get people to come and look at the paintings. With a bit of publicity you'll get more people coming and we'll all get more feedback and maybe even more paintings bought."

She could hear him sigh deeply as their feet trod the dark road. "I know you're right. Maybe I am a purist. Perhaps that's why I'm a better painter and a better teacher than I am a businessman. Here's your gate. Are you going to ask me in?"

"I'm not. I've got a lot to think about and so have you. See you in class." Her torch caught the bulk of him as he stood looking dejected. "Goodnight my good friend."

12
———

Alison saw them in a bookshop. She was buying birthday cards and hoping to pick up information on charities when she noticed them. They were paperbacks in a row and above them a cardboard cut-out proclaiming a local hero. She looked at the titles. *Air Commando One. When The Sky Was Pitiless. Alpha Bravo. Desert Wings. Challenge and Command.* All by Hal Davidson. Intrigued, she picked one up and looked at the biography of the writer and the list of previous publications. She read the synopsis on the back cover, and slipped it into her basket with the other shopping. The young man at the checkout nodded his approval.

"Great book, that one. But they're all really wicked."

THE BOOK LAY on the hall table and she passed it several times before she picked it up to look at it. From the back cover she learned that the story was one of danger, risk, action and heroism and that the writer, like the hero in the book, had known risk, danger, action and heroism. She found the opening compelling and the writing quickly drew her into the action in what was clearly a man's world. But when the action became violence she stopped reading and sat quietly, thinking about the writer, about herself, about what on earth had made her buy this book. Then she resolutely closed it and determined that this was the first and last she would buy but at least now her picture of the man in the wheelchair was illuminated. So that was his world. Action man. No sensitivity; no gentleness; no appreciation of the many small joys of ordinary things. This was a violent and brutalised warrior clearly furious with a fate that prevented him flying his war machine and confined him to a wheelchair and that ridiculous Trailblazer. Unable to blaze a trail across the sky anymore, his bitterness spilled out in discourtesy and his damaged macho ego offered nothing but worthless put-downs.

From the back cover, the image of David looked directly at her. As though compelled, she gazed back into the serious grey eyes and remembered the brief glint of a smile she'd seen and the dispirited clouding of his face as he sat, pinned to his sofa, the only softness in his hard-edged masculine environment. Was there no woman in his life? Not that one would stay for long with the overbearing, humourless, insensitive attitudes he had. She stood up suddenly and tossed the book into a basket of catalogues and magazines.

VOICES BOUNCED about the high-vaulted ceiling of Alison's sitting room as Aidan's committee gathered. She put another log into the wood-burning stove and Virginia and Aidan passed round glasses of wine and Virginia's renowned cheesy biscuits.

"I can never get mine like this, Virginia. You gave me the recipe ages ago, remember? I sometimes wonder if you wrote it down correctly." Janet looked over her glasses at Virginia.

"Maybe it's my Aga," said Virginia tartly.

"Ladies, ladies," Aidan sipped his wine and placed the glass on the mantelpiece. He pushed his hands into the pockets of his ancient cord trousers, rose up on his toes and down again, leaned slightly forward and said, "So nice that everyone is here. The whole class. Such enthusiasm and so gratifying. Before we look at the nuts and bolts of our exhibition, I'm going to ask Alison to fill us in on her charity. Over to you." Aidan reclaimed his glass and folded himself into the only spare chair.

"This isn't my charity," Alison shot an irritated glance at Aidan, "but I hope it could be something we might all feel involved with. I feel so fortunate every time I turn on a tap and without fail there's clean water. In parts of Africa, a child dies every fifteen seconds as a result of poor water. And for many women and girls, much of their day is spent fetching water, water which may bring disease. The charity I hope we might all support is Cleanwater and here are some leaflets I've gathered about it, if you'd be kind enough to pass them round. It brings local solutions to local problems. The whole community is involved in building tanks and laying pipes and the result can be that a five-mile walk becomes a five-minute queue for safe water. It seems to me that if our exhibition and the work we put into it can result in fewer children dying from dirty water and whole communities being free from lethal water-borne diseases, it'll be well worth our time and effort." Alison smiled encouragingly as the sparrows rustled their leaflets and nodded.

"The meeting is open for discussion," Aidan drawled. "Clearly as we're all working towards the same objective we need to reach agreement eventually, however long and arduous the discussion might be." He refilled his glass and settled back in his chair prepared for discussion. No voices of dissent came.

"I tried to make sure everyone had all the information I could lay my hands on before this evening," murmured Alison, "and there has already been much discussion."

"Good," said Aidan, surprised. "Well, if we're in agreement, let's get on, shall we?"

. . .

ALISON'S FINGERS began to irritably fiddle with her pen as the
meeting dragged on. The endless repetition and discussion of
minutiae was getting to her. She could do all this herself in half
the time.

"What about the celebrity to open the exhibition?" The
voice came from the far end of the sofa.

"Oh. I've had a brainwave." It was Henry. Everyone turned
to look at him. "What about Hal Davidson? You know, David
Rowbottom? He's a celebrity and right here in the village."

Alison's heart sank. No way, she thought, absolutely
no way.

"It's a good idea, Henry, but he's not awfully fit just now, is
he, Virginia?" she said, looking meaningfully at Virginia.

"But we're talking months ahead, Alison, and David will be
starting intensive physiotherapy shortly so we're actually all
being very positive," said Virginia.

"Do you mean, he might be able to, you know, I'm sorry, I
shouldn't, didn't…" a hesitant voice faded.

"It's all right," Virginia smiled kindly at the hesitant
speaker, "we just have to take each day at a time. That's what
David does so we do too. But we can but ask. Would you like
me to ask him?"

"Well it's no good me asking him," muttered Alison. "I'd be
sure to get a no."

"Sorry Alison, what was that?"

"Nothing. I was really thinking more of a 'bling' celebrity,
you know, a footballer or a television personality."

"But David is a celebrity."

As Virginia said the words, Alison had had enough. "Virginia, I have never heard of David Rowbottom or Hal
Davidson."

"That's because you haven't been living in this country.

David is a decorated hero, a top bestselling writer and a tireless campaigner for people who are disabled, especially servicemen. He was on that excellent programme on BBC2 and he master-minded that rally and got all those funds together for the hospital that rehabilitates servicemen. Huge publicity. Of course he's a celebrity."

Virginia glared at Alison and everyone else in the room did the same. Alison looked at Aidan, who slowly shrugged his shoulders and sipped his wine. She felt herself flushing. This whole thing was becoming fraught with difficulty. She knew she was looking at defeat. And then she smiled. She had the answer.

"OK," she said lightly, "I'll ask him, shall I?" And the voice within her said he's bound to say no to me. "Perhaps we could talk, Virginia, and you could just help me with a few things, like how to make my approach?" Her smile was sweet and her expression innocent. "Maybe lunch? Tomorrow? The Italian place in Fordingham."

THE NICE THING about Diego's was that the chairs were comfortable with plenty of cushions you could use or discard and a table in a corner meant you could talk without the competition of many voices in the main room. Alison was already suitably cushioned with a glass of rosé when Virginia arrived, all frenetic haste, shopping bags and unruly hair. Alison silently sipped her rosé as Virginia got out of her coat, stashed her bags and sorted the cushions on her chair.

"A glass of pink, Virginia?"

"A stiff gin would do me more good, but let it be pink. There is still much ahead of me." Her look was grim.

"Nothing wrong, I hope?"

"Oh no." She smiled her thanks as the waiter supplied the rosé. "Just the dog to get to the vet, my hoover to collect from

Digby's, the Parish newsletter to deliver and Robert's aunt to visit in hospital, with, of course, her clean laundry." Virginia smiled valiantly at Alison, every hair on her head electric with irritation.

Alison looked at her with affection. "You're so good, Virginia. Always doing things for other people."

"No I'm not. But anyway, what else do you do? Things need doing and I can do them."

"So can Robert."

"Don't go down that road. It's pointless. My life would be infinitely more difficult if I tried to change him now. It's best just to get on with things. Anyway, maybe I like being useful."

"Well useful you certainly are, especially to me," Alison said briskly. "Let's order and then I can pump you for information. I've told you before that I really think your brother-in-law finds me the most irritating individual on this earth. That's the way he makes me feel, anyway. And if I'm honest, the feeling is mutual. But I can put up with that if you really think his appearance at a gala opening will bring people to this exhibition and help us with the fundraising. Really and truly. Sentiment apart. And if you think he'll be fit enough."

Virginia skilfully forked her pasta before replying. "You'll have to do the asking. As for his celebrity, I have no doubt he'll attract numbers. His private life is something he guards jealously but when he's campaigning or doing book tours he makes quite a stir. Highvale is his home and I think there'll be a bit of a cachet there, you know, Hal Davidson's home town. I would imagine you'll have to work on him from the charity angle."

"I don't want to work on him, Virginia. Either he agrees to do this willingly or we forget it. For heaven's sake, there are plenty of other people I can approach."

"Oh really? And who did you have in mind?"

"Well, what about someone like Charlie Pentarron?"

"The rock star? You know him?"

"An acquaintance, but Nick sees him all the time. And Giselle has really famous clients, you know, truly bling and in *Hello Magazine* all the time."

"Mmmm." Virginia stirred her coffee. "Do your children mind you using their contacts like this?"

"I don't particularly mind if they mind. This is for a good cause."

"Then I suggest you get over your antipathy to David and ask him to do it. For a good cause."

"What about his fitness then, I mean is it fair to ask someone in a wheelchair to do this?"

"Ah well," Virginia was gathering up her bags. "The only person to answer that is David. You'll just have to ask him. Here's the number." She ripped the page out of a small notebook. Alison pushed back her chair and bashed the cushions back into place as she left. Hell and damnation, she thought, shouldering her bag and putting up her umbrella as she headed out into the rain. I'm just trying to do something worthwhile here in my privileged and sheltered life and all I get is aggro.

13

A lison looked balefully at Nick when he slouched into the kitchen just after dawn.

"My God, mother. You're up early." He took a juice carton from the fridge and drank from it.

"For heaven's sake, Nick, use a glass!"

He put some bread in the toaster and grabbed a plate.

"Why are you up so early? I've got to get off to Goodwood. Bloody miles."

Alison morosely sipped her coffee in silence.

"So?" Nick retrieved the toast.

"So what?"

"So why are you up so early?"

"I couldn't sleep, if you must know."

"Problems? Plants not coming up as they should or is it the painting? Can't get the perspective right?"

"Well, really!" Alison's mug resounded on the worktop. "I do have other things going on in my life, you know."

"Do you? But I thought you liked the gardening and the painting."

"Yes, but that's not all my life's about." She saw Nick's troubled look and was instantly remorseful. "I'm sorry. It's not your fault. It's perfectly understandable that you think I'm content to just sit here and be comfortably domestic, especially after the pain I went through, we all went through."

Nick shifted uncomfortably. "I thought you were all right now, Mum. Ed and I both thought you'd done really well to pull through and make a new life for yourself, you know, settle down at last after all that moving from place to place."

Alison wearily pushed her hair from her eyes and perched on the kitchen stool. "I am, really. It's just that I've got a bit of a challenge and I'm disappointed to find that perhaps I'm not quite as up for it as I thought I was."

"Want to talk about it?" Nick asked generously, his lopsided grin tugging at her heart.

She smiled. "No, darling. But thank you for the offer. You have to get to Goodwood and all I have to do is grow up. And toughen up." She held herself erect and looked up at her tall son who took another sip from the orange juice carton and put it back in the fridge.

"Great. Mind if I use the bathroom first?"

THE CHALLENGE SEEMED to grow larger as the days went by. Virginia's small piece of paper with David's number on it was like a beacon by the phone, catching her eye every time she passed. The date of the next meeting grew nearer and Alison knew she must bite the bullet and make the call. She chose early evening, supportive glass of wine nearby, and punched the numbers into the phone.

"David Rowbottom." The voice was impatient.

"Good evening. It's Alison Henderson. I do hope I'm not disturbing you, but there's something I'd like to ask you." Why did she sound so formal? "I mean, it'll need explaining of course, and possibly it's not your thing at all…" her voice fluttered and ceased and she gripped the phone as the silence grew. "This is ridiculous," she muttered. Silence. "Are you still there?"

"Just."

"I don't normally behave like this."

"Like what? You mean you don't normally phone men in the early evening to ask them something?"

"Oh here we go again. No, that's not at all what I mean. I mean when I need to ask someone something I usually just ask."

"Well then, why don't you just ask?"

"Because it's complicated, and, well, unlike some people I do have a regard for the feelings of others."

"Oh don't worry, I am well aware how worthy you are."

"Worthy! What do you mean, worthy? You think I'm some do-gooder do you?"

"It's really immaterial what I think, isn't it?"

"This conversation is going nowhere." She took a slug of wine. So why don't I just put the phone down? She listened to the silence. She willed herself to say nothing. He didn't disconnect. The silence became something she could feel. She held her breath. Suddenly she heard a chuckle.

"You could come round and ask me." The phone went dead. He'd put it down. Come round? Go there? When? Now? She straightened her back, squared her shoulders and raised her chin. OK then, she would. She'd go now. Time to get this over with.

ALISON SLIPPED ON HER COAT, picked up her Art Exhibition file, grabbed her car keys and closed the door firmly behind her.

Her headlights lit up the wet road as she turned into The Glebe and pulled up behind the Trailblazer. Clutching her file, she headed for the key safe behind the down pipe. It wasn't there. Was this the right pipe? She bent closer, feeling the smooth pipe and the rough brick in the dark. A car drove past, slowing down as she was caught in its headlights. Quickly she straightened up. The key safe must be in a new place. She'd just have to ring the bell and call through the letterbox.

"Hellooooo," she called, bent double with fingers in the letterbox. Suddenly the door opened, pulling her into the house where she crashed into a wheelchair and found herself on her knees with her head in David Rowbottom's lap. The laughter started before she lifted her head; muffled laughter into his lap, peals of laughter as she collapsed backwards onto her heels, helpless tear-streaming laughter when she leant back on her hands. David pushed the door shut. Helplessly she looked up at him. He turned the wheels of his chair and backed off, his solemn expression fracturing as his mouth curved to smile. Alison stopped laughing, her head on one side looking at him, her cheeks wet with the tears of her laughter. The silence lengthened and both were motionless. Suddenly Alison started to laugh again, collapsing onto the floor where she limply subsided and lay full length, arms out, fingers feeling the smooth cold wood. She took a deep breath as her laughter ceased.

Quietly, he spoke. "Are you OK?"

"I'm gathering myself," she said, her eyes shut, blotting out the quiet man above her. The smell of floor polish mingled with his limey coriander freshness. She sniffed. No smell of hospitals.

"Gathering yourself for what?"

"For standing up. There is no way to stand up elegantly from this undignified position."

"Is it necessary to be elegant or dignified?"

"Oh yes, it certainly is. It's essential. I have come here on a serious mission to impress you so I can ask you a favour and thus far my score is zero. Still, I don't suppose you'll forget my entrance in a hurry. At least that will have impressed you. Well, the only way is up."

She opened her eyes. David rolled his chair towards her and held out his hand.

"Let me help you," he said gravely. Surprised, she put out her hand and felt the strength of his grasp and the force of his steadying pull as he helped her, releasing her hand once she was steady. He turned the chair and headed towards the living room. "Coming?" he asked over his shoulder. Alison picked up her file and scattered papers, pulled down her cardigan and followed him, stopping and turning back to the hall again to retrieve the shoe she'd left behind.

DAVID WAS IN THE KITCHEN, pulling a bottle of wine from the fridge.

"Have a seat, Mrs Henderson."

Alison sat on the big tan sofa, placed the file beside her and crossed her legs.

"Oh please," she said, waving a hand elegantly, "don't call me Mrs Henderson. Call me Madam."

Her heart skipped at his shout of laughter. He spun his chair to face her and advanced, a tray with two glasses of wine on his lap.

"Madam," he said, offering the tray. She took a glass and smiled at his amusement.

"Merry," she said. "A word we only tend to use at Christmas, but when you laugh you look really merry."

He looked shocked. "Merry. How can you say that to me?

Merry is pink cheeks and jollity. That's as bad as me calling you worthy."

"What are you then, if you're not merry?"

"Oh, let's see. I think the words that best describe me are elegant and dignified." He smiled and raised his glass. "Now, about that question."

"Oh yes." She put her glass on the table beside her and reached for her file. "Goodness, must get back to reality. It's quite weird, really, talking amicably with you and laughing with you."

David looked at her, head back, eyes half closed. "Well, when someone at last gets off their high horse it makes a difference." She stiffened. He held up his hand, as though defending himself. "Your question, Madam?"

Alison sat upright, looking at him seriously. "I'm going to be honest from the outset because that's the best way to be, don't you think?"

"Definitely."

"Well I know you have had difficulty with health issues, not that I know any details at all and why should I? None of my business and everyone quite rightly is bound by the strictest code of confidentiality. So I'm going to ask you this favour and please just say no if you feel you're unable to manage it."

David shifted in his wheelchair. "Go on."

She looked at him doubtfully, feeling nervous and detecting a cooling between them. Why was she nervous? She wanted him to say no, didn't she?

"Well, what this is about is two things, one very close to my heart and the other not without its importance too."

David put his hand on his heart. "Let's do the heart bit first." She watched as he smiled, his face lighting up, his eyes crinkling, his mouth twitching slightly at one corner as though he were restraining a laugh.

"Are you laughing at me?"

He put down his glass and propelled his chair closer.

"Actually, I'm not. I can see you have something you really care about to say and I honestly respect that. So go ahead."

And she did. She told him about the pain she felt when she saw the pictures of starving children on the news; how she remembered witnessing people struggling to grow crops when the rains failed; how pointless her life seemed at times when her own personal amusement seemed to be the only thing filling her days. She told him about Cleanwater, handing him her leaflets and walking up and down in front of him, emphasising the importance of involving the people in need so their dignity is respected and they can take over the project themselves.

"So when Aidan…"

"Aidan? Who's Aidan?"

"He's a painter. Lives the other side of the Village Green and he has this painting class. Surely you know who Aidan is. Aidan thought it would be good for us to…"

"Us? You go to this class?"

"I do." Why did he keep interrupting her? "We are going to have an exhibition of paintings. Initially it was just a small endeavour but suddenly it occurred to me that we might raise some funds for Cleanwater. If we did that, I felt I'd be happy to spend time working at some painting."

"Will you show me your pictures?"

"If you like. I don't expect they'll be to your taste," she lifted an arm and indicated the big, airy skies of David's pictures high on the walls, "but it's something I enjoy doing and Aidan thinks I'm improving."

"Does he now."

"I'm coming to the tricky bit now." She sat down and leaned earnestly towards him. "You see, if we're going to do this I think we should do it as big time as we can, make it really good, even if it is just the Village Hall, and raise as much money as we can and I, we, wondered if you would be kind enough to come to a gala evening and be the guest celebrity who opens the exhibition."

He picked up his glass, taking a sip in silence, swirling the cold clear liquid around the glass, looking at her through it. "Why did you think this was the tricky bit?"

"Because I don't know how well you are and I don't know what you feel about your celebrity or about other people using your celebrity."

"I am not an invalid."

"I can see that now. But last time I saw you, you were not as able as you are now. In fact, you were practically pinned to this sofa and I had no way of knowing how your recovery was going. I just had to risk it and ask you."

"What were you risking?"

Surprised by the question, Alison paused. What had she been risking?

"Well, I suppose the risk was that you'd say no."

"Not much of a risk, that, surely. There are plenty of people you could approach."

"I don't know what I was risking," she muttered. "A lot of the time I don't understand myself at all."

David topped up the glasses. His voice was deep when he said, "Sometimes things happen to us; life throws things at us that we don't understand. Understanding isn't necessarily required. You just have to get on with stuff no matter what." His face was grim and his knuckles white as his hand gripped the glass but his cool grey eyes looked at her steadily as he waited for her reply.

"So will you do it? Will you open this exhibition?" Tensely she waited for him to speak. You fool, she thought, you came to ask him because you were sure that he would say no. You can't possibly be hoping he'll say yes.

At last he spoke. "This isn't something I normally do. But perhaps you could convince me why I should."

He put the glass down carefully, folded his hands in his lap and watched her quietly. His body was still, composed, a powerful image in spite of the matt black metal of the wheelchair supporting him. He seemed to Alison like a cat, like a black panther, muscles coiled, waiting to spring. She remembered the words of cruelty and violence she'd read in his book. She felt the edginess of the room around her, the hard shiny floor, the stark white walls, the cold chrome of the kitchen at the edge of her vision slicing away all comfort and she sat alert, wary, suspicious. Her laughter at her ridiculous arrival was long gone. There was nothing to laugh at now and she knew it would be better if David declined. The less she saw of this man the better. She stood up to leave.

"Thank you for the wine. I completely understand that this sort of thing is not for you. It was good of you to listen to me." She picked up her file and smiled tightly.

David was motionless. Then he smiled a wide, sweet, gentle smile and said quietly, "May I come and see your paintings?"

"My paintings? Whatever for?"

"Because I'm interested."

"But you can't be."

"Why can't I be?"

"I don't know why. Because they aren't what would interest you, I suppose."

"You can't possibly know what interests me."

"Well, I do. Vehicles and planes and macho things are surely what interest you. War. Combat. My paintings aren't like that at all."

"Well show me, then." His voice was quiet.

She looked at him helplessly. "How?"

"Ask me round. I'll come over."

"I'll need to think about it, look at my diary…"

"Fine." He spun the chair and headed for the hall. "I'll wait for your call." He opened the door and she walked past him into the night.

"Goodnight," she said.

"Goodnight," and before he closed the door she heard him say, "Madam."

14

Pale sunshine slanted through the windows of the Village Hall as Aidan's art group unpacked their brushes, paper and paints. Alison dumped her bag on a free table with a sigh and unzipped it. She hoped she'd remembered everything. She felt tired and low-spirited. She was uncertain about the Art Exhibition. Her idea that she could effectively contribute to a major humanitarian problem now seemed ridiculous and completely unrealistic. Since her meeting with David, her whole life had felt disorganised and chaotic. So annoying. She'd forgotten to leave the key out for Jake last Thursday; failed to keep a dental appointment and posted Sally's birthday card late. She leafed through her paintings, half a dozen large sheets of paper, putting one carefully on top of the other. Where was the one she was working on? Hell and damnation. She'd left it on her easel at home. Hands on hips, she looked crossly at the pile of paper.

"Problem?" Aidan looked amused as he leant on the other side of the table. Alison felt instant irritation.

"I've left the painting I was working on at home. I'll have to go back for it." She turned her back on him, grabbed her jacket and car keys and left the hall. The door swung shut behind her. She could see her small yellow car on the other side of the road. Behind it loomed the black mass of the Trailblazer. She hesitated, aware that her heart was suddenly racing. I really don't like this, she thought. I really don't like feeling rattled and irritable and disorganised. Standing still outside the Village Hall, she looked hard at the Trailblazer to see if David was in it. Oh this was silly. She crossed the road and the engine of the Trailblazer started up. A window lowered. David waved.

"Hello there. I'm just off. You'll find it easier to pull out when I've gone." His engine kicked into gear and the vehicle had swung out into the road and left before she had her car door open.

SHE FELT the sun disappear and light rain begin to fall as she sank into her car and pulled the door shut, angrily shoving the key into the ignition. Alison's hands gripped the steering wheel and she stared silently up the road, now empty of Trailblazers. It's David, she thought. He's a malign influence. There is absolutely nothing about that man which is connected in any way to anything pleasant or joyful or even helpful. He is clearly completely self-absorbed, has a brooding heaviness of spirit that I find hugely unattractive, even threatening. I really don't want to have anything more to do with him. She thrust the car into gear and drove home to pick up her painting. She'd have a word with Aidan when she got back. She would tell him this idea of David opening the exhibition was not going to work and then she needn't have anything more to do with him. What was the point when the man made her feel so uncomfortable?

THE CLASS ENDED and Alison told Virginia she didn't think she could work with David.

"Oh dear. You sound really cross. What's he done?"

"Well, nothing really. I mean, it's not something he's done exactly it's just that I don't think we get on."

"But you don't need to 'get on', Alison. All we want him to do is open the exhibition."

"It'll be more than that, Virginia. He'll have to support the charity, promote the event in advance, be part of the publicity before and after it, hand the cheque over, that sort of thing."

"Well, let him do all that. You don't have to do it with him."

"But this is what I wanted to do. I wanted to support this charity and be involved and everything."

"What's more important, Alison, you doing the supporting or the charity benefitting from the support we're all giving it?" Virginia's look was determined.

Alison sighed deeply. "You're right. I'm sorry. Things are a bit confusing just now. This is so unlike me." She laughed a dry, brittle laugh. "You'd think, wouldn't you, that someone of my age and with my experience of the world would be more on top of things than this."

"You look so upset." Virginia put her arm round Alison's shoulders. "Come home with me. Come and tell me all about it. This isn't anything major. I'm sure there'll be a simple solution."

Alison shook her head. "I won't. Thanks Virginia. I'm fine. Really. As you say, it's nothing major." She picked up her brushes and slid them one by one into their compartments, zipping her case as the hall emptied.

"Alison, just a word please." Aidan smiled and picked up her board with the painting taped to it. "Coming along well. Don't you agree?"

"I suppose so."

"Only suppose? You can be more certain than that." He put the painting down. "This is looking good to me. The lines are excellent and your painting is lovely and loose; good clear colour. I wouldn't do any more to that, if I were you. Frame it as it is."

She nodded, looking at her painting of the little tree in her garden. She looked at the framework of skeletal branches she'd drawn reaching out into a brooding winter sky. As she'd drawn them she'd appreciated their delicacy and the shape they gave to the tree. She remembered the care she'd taken to get the roundness of barely visible buds and the liveliness of the birds swooping to the hanging coconut shell; the inspiration she'd had from the pale, bare scene and the sense of achievement that she'd managed to mix the subtle colours and kept them clear and translucent.

"This is lovely, Alison. In spite of its delicacy it has a vitality, a power. I really like it. Don't look at me like that, with your eyebrows raised in disbelief. I mean it."

"Really?"

"Really. This is one of the best things you've done."

Alison squinted at the picture, a thought slowly dawning. "Aidan, I feel really excited that you think this is a reasonably good painting…"

"Alison," he interrupted her, picking up the board with the painting on it and leaning it against the wall, "in my view it isn't to do with a judgement, labelling this one as good, this one poor, stuff like that. Paintings say what they say; they're individual. They speak with their own voices. Some pictures are competent and correct and wonderfully decorative but that's all. Now, in my view this is a very nice watercolour, competently drawn and painted but it has a voice. I haven't seen you achieve that before. It certainly is nothing to do with anything I taught you. It's not something anyone can teach. A person has to find their own voice and I think, in this picture, you've found yours. Remember when we were looking at my painting of your Stables, how we spoke about pictures communicating?"

Alison nodded. "I do remember. You said you were a communicator not a decorator."

"Precisely. This picture is communicating to me. Don't you see? I can see the fragility of this tree in the winter, the fragility of life, the sense of loss of the bare branches and yet, here are the buds, the hope of new life, and the birds, valiantly sustaining their lives as do the snowdrops for whom winter is a time to bloom joyfully. It has mixed emotions; feelings of loss and vulnerability underpinned with the beginnings of hope and a glimpse of joy." Aidan turned from the painting and looked silently at Alison.

She looked steadily back at him, amazement creeping over her. He had not only described her painting but her own feelings. He understood her so well.

"Let me cook supper for you," he said. "Come home with me after the pub."

She nodded, smiling. "That would be lovely. Thank you."

"Right. Let's go. The Huntsman and a good glass of claret await."

FOR ALISON, the warmth and chatter of the gathering in The Huntsman was intermittently shot through with the clear sharp needles of knowledge given to her by Aidan's expert and positive critique of her painting. From across the room she caught a glimpse of herself in the smoky old mirror above the fire, face flushed and eyes sparkling, her excitement apparent. Maybe, just maybe, she'd found something of her own that she could do well. She watched Aidan, laidback and laconic; carelessly loose limbed and untidy, surrounded by his sparrows. But what sensitive insight he'd shown. Had he realized he'd been describing her own feelings when he talked about her painting? She found herself hoping he had.

. . .

SITTING in a comfortable battered old chair in Aidan's kitchen, Alison watched as he put crusty bread in the oven to warm, washed a lettuce and some tomatoes and beat some eggs.

"You haven't stopped smiling all evening." He spoke with his back to her, putting a frying pan on a hotplate.

Alison laughed. "Haven't I? I am extraordinarily pleased with your critique of my painting. I feel like a child who's had a gold star."

"Well, it is a bit of a breakthrough. Up to the table now. Omelette aux fines herbes, du pain et du salade await."

LOOKING at Aidan across empty plates, empty glasses and two big cups of coffee, Alison found the chaos and character of his kitchen and the creativity of his life and personality had soothed her, comforted and uplifted her. She felt all things were possible.

"Thank you for this evening. I feel cared about and valued and it's lovely."

"Don't tell me you've been feeling uncared for and unvalued? Surely not, with your lovely sons and your friend Virginia keeping an eye on you." Aidan leaned back theatrically.

"Well to be honest I don't know quite what's been going on recently, but I certainly haven't felt full of the joys. Felt a bit lost, really. Directionless."

"Well that's bad news for the Exhibition Committee; pretty bad news for Cleanwater too, if the chief fundraiser is feeling directionless."

"But now, extraordinarily, thanks to you, I feel energised. I think what you recognised in my painting was passion and intent and I was thinking about hope in hard times when I was doing it. I do passionately want to get this funding together for Cleanwater."

"Then where's the problem?"

"There isn't one. I'll tackle it head on."

"There is no problem and you'll tackle it head on. Why doesn't that make sense to me?" His laughter joined Alison's.

"There is an issue I will tackle head on but I'm not going to spoil a lovely evening and my excitement about my picture by even thinking about it, let alone mentioning it. Aidan, thank you for being my friend, for understanding me so well and for your expert tuition and encouragement."

His chair scraped on the tiled floor as he stood up and came round the table, taking her hands and bringing her to her feet. He wrapped her in his arms, cradling her head and smoothing her hair. "You've come such a long way." She felt him rock her gently. "You were like a hurt bird, fragile and beautiful with a fearful and wary look and now you're strong again, no longer fearful and you'll fly and share your strength and your beauty my darling. No, no, don't stiffen like that. Trust me. You are my darling, right now you are my darling friend, and please remember you can always depend on me."

Alison allowed the tenderness of his touch and his words to envelop her and found herself simply receiving the affection of this talented and kind man. She felt grateful for the honesty of the moment and the easing of her loneliness.

15

Alison woke with alarm. The phone was ringing. It was dark. Something was wrong. She sat up in bed and reached for the phone.

"Hello?"

"Mrs Henderson?"

"Yes. Yes, this is Mrs Henderson." Her other hand found its way to the phone, steadying it. In the dark she waited.

"Mrs Henderson, it's Kellie-Ann. I'm calling you for Nick. I had a call just now and his phone was running out of battery and he asked me to call you."

"Oh. I see." The fright diminished a little. "Go on."

"He said he'd told you he'd be back tonight and didn't want you to worry. He's had to go over to France suddenly and then he'll be tied up at Pentarron's, he says. He'll call as soon as he's managed to get a network and charge his phone." Alison snapped on her bedside light and looked at her watch. It was a little past one in the morning.

"Thank you, Kellie-Ann. But I wasn't worried. Why should I be worried?"

"No idea. But I just had the call and Nick said to be sure you're not worried. So that's what I did."

"Well that's really thoughtful and I appreciate it. When he calls again please tell him everything's OK. I'm OK."

"OK. 'Bye."

"'Bye." She put down the phone and switched off the light. Nick was nearly thirty. Why should he suddenly get it into his head that she would worry about him? She hauled the duvet up and rolled over, acknowledging to herself she hadn't really taken it on board that he'd said he'd be back tonight. Lying warm in the dark she smiled at his thoughtfulness and as her mind dwelt on Nick it occurred to her that faced with a tiny amount of battery left it was Kellie-Ann he'd called; Kellie-Ann whose voice he'd wanted to hear; Kellie-Ann who must first be reassured.

To her surprise, the next day Kellie-Ann appeared at the front door of The Stables.

"Hi there." Kellie-Ann was enveloped in an orange anorak, hood thrown back, hair neatly tied and smile dazzling.

"Kellie-Ann, what a surprise." Alison held open the door. "Come in."

Kellie-Ann nimbly entered and kicked off the tiniest flattest ballet pumps Alison had ever seen and which were in complete contradiction to the vast orange anorak. She shrugged off the anorak and hooked it on a coat peg. She went into the kitchen, slid onto a stool, leaned against the granite and beamed at Alison.

"Coffee?" Alison switched on the kettle.

"I'd love a mint tea if you have one."

"D'you know I don't, but I do have a Rooibos. Would that be of interest? I have them for Jake, who helps me with the garden."

"OK then. Go for it."

Alison went for it, and a high-caffeine coffee for herself.

"So, Kellie-Ann. How are things for you?"

"Great, thanks, Mrs Henderson."

"Do you think we might drop the Mrs Henderson? Alison would do."

Kellie-Ann shifted on the stool and re-crossed her legs, wiggled her bare, cranberry-tipped toes, sipped her tea and put down the mug. "OK then. Alison. The tea's OK too."

"So life's great. I'm glad." Alison allowed the silence between them to lengthen.

"How are things for you? Alison?" Kellie-Ann was tentative.

"Well Kellie-Ann, as you see I have no apparent difficulties and I'm involved with this and that in the village and my grandchildren are well and spring is on the way which means an exciting time in the garden and I have quite a lot to do, what with painting and getting ready for this exhibition we're having in the Village Hall and..."

"Oh yes. I've heard about that," interrupted Kellie-Ann.

"Oh really? We haven't done any publicity yet. How did you hear?"

"Oh, I dunno. Can't remember. So you've got a bit to do?"

Alison smiled and put her coffee mug firmly on the granite. "Kellie-Ann it's lovely to see you, but was there a reason why you came this morning?"

"No. None at all." Kellie-Ann's eyes were wide. She glanced at her big round wrist watch. "Ooh. Have to dash. I'm just here on a break."

"On a break? What sort of break?"

"Working." Kellie-Ann indicated her navy trousers and tunic.

"So working in the village." They looked at one another. "Kellie-Ann, why don't you tell me why you really came?"

Kellie-Ann slid off her stool and rinsed her mug under the tap, setting it carefully on the draining board and smiling brightly.

"How is your garden coming along, Alison? Could I have a quick look?"

"A quick look? What do you mean, a quick look? You want me to give you a tour of my garden?"

"No, no, not a tour. Can I just look through your big windows?"

"Well of course you can. Come this way." Alison led Kellie-Ann through the lofty sitting room to the big arched windows at the end. Kellie-Ann padded along behind her. Side by side they stood and looked out at the dripping little tree, the neat row of brown, desiccated herbaceous plants along the path and the empty trellises against the old brick wall. Alison glanced sideways at Kellie-Ann. Why this sudden interest in her garden? She saw Kellie-Ann narrow her eyes looking at the garden door in the far wall and again as she focussed through the big glass door in front of them on the pathway immediately the other side of the glass.

"So there you are, Kellie-Ann. My garden. All twigs and good earth and huge potential."

Kellie-Ann nodded vigorously. "Oh yes. Certainly potential," she breathed. "Well, better dash. Thanks a bunch." And Kellie-Ann was off, feet slipped into the ballet pumps, shrouded in the vast anorak and out of the front door, waving cheerfully. Her tiny red car coughed into life and she was gone.

Alison slowly closed the door and gave up the struggle for comprehension. Just accept, she said to herself. You can't live the lives of others and neither can you live your life through them. Whatever's going on with Kellie-Ann and Nick is their business. I have to live my own life. The phone rang. It was Giselle. The children had chickenpox.

"Alison, can you come? They're not too bad but of course I

can't leave them and I'd be so grateful for Tuesday and Wednesday."

"Of course I'll come. I just need to be back for Friday. A meeting for an exhibition."

SHE KEPT the volume of the radio low as she drove. The traffic report would kick in loudly enough. It was pleasant being enclosed in the car, driving with a purpose. She felt better than she had for ages; felt she was in the right place doing the right thing. Aidan's encouragement made her look forward with enjoyable anticipation to starting her next painting and his friendship was heartwarming. There was just the issue of David to sort out, or should I say Hal Davidson, she thought. And instantly, like a breeze which ripples still water, she found her contentment disturbed. I just won't go down that road, she thought, skilfully coming off the motorway and up the slip road. I'll do a Scarlett O'Hara and think about that tomorrow.

"OH CHLOE DARLING," she received Chloe's hug and held her at arm's length, "look at you, my sweetheart. Well, you're not so bad, are you? Just a few little spots and they'll soon be gone. Come, let's get my stuff inside and you can tell me all about it. Where's Toby?"

"He's doing his Lego."

Alison took Chloe's hand and kissed Giselle. "Well, how convenient to have them both down with chickenpox at the same time. Yes please, a cup of tea would be lovely." Alison was absorbed into the world of the children, pleased to divert and comfort them and give their mother some space. She sat on the floor in the playroom, enjoying the jumble of toys, coloured chalks on the blackboard, a half completed jigsaw on a little table, Toby lying on the floor creating a space station. Chloe nestled on the floor beside her, pale face with scabby spots upturned, and offered Alison a large colourful storybook.

"Toby, when we've read this

story do you think you could give me a tour of your space station? It looks really interesting." She sipped her tea and smiled at the little boy who was unusually quiet and looked so like his father with his straight dark hair which fell forwards just as his father's did. And his grandfather's. James suddenly invaded her thoughts. Did he ever see or have news of his grandchildren? She remembered Ed with chickenpox, but she seemed to recall he'd made much more of a fuss. Ed! Nick! She hadn't thought to tell Nick she wasn't at home. She'd text him and keep fingers crossed he'd hit a network somewhere sometime.

CURLED IN A CHAIR, feet tucked under her, Giselle sat opposite Alison in front of the fire. Bedtime was over, the children soothed and sleeping. Padded curtains, heavy and pale and hanging immaculately from massive shiny cream curtain poles, were drawn across the full width of the windows in the elegant living room. The firelight played with textures and shadows and Alison felt absorbed into the room's carefully designed comfort. So different from David's house. There were no hard edges here, no expanses of cold shininess, no brushed aluminium, no regimented ranks of books. Like turning a page, she resolutely tried to put David out of her mind.

The firelight flickered across a row of pretty ivory silk cushions and threw into relief Giselle's generous rounded chairs and sofas and Alison drew round her a sense of wellbeing.

"What time do you expect Ed?"

"Soon. As you're here he said he'd get back earlier."

"Lovely. Sure there's nothing you'd like me to do for supper?"

"No. It's all ready. Just relax. Tell me, how are you? How's life in Highvale?"

"You're looking at me speculatively, Giselle."

"Well, you look different from the last time I saw you and I can't put my finger on it. You haven't changed your hair. I don't think you've lost weight. You don't look tense or anxious. But something's different."

"Well, I don't know what it could be. Are you accustomed to being so closely observant?" Alison felt rattled.

"Oh yes. I have to be. Interpreting what people want is very important in my world. They tell you what they want and they think that is indeed what they do want but I observe an awful lot. I can identify what it is they really want and offer it to them." Giselle effortlessly uncurled and stood up. "Tiny top-up?" She held out her hand for Alison's glass.

"So if you did some interpreting of me, what do you think I really want?"

"Not the right time to say. Your life has changed so dramatically and traumatically so recently and you need time for everything to settle." Giselle smiled sweetly and glided off to the kitchen. Again, Alison felt irritation nibble at the edges of her sense of wellbeing. Was Giselle presuming that she could see what was right for Alison, something Alison couldn't even see for herself? She hardly knew her, not as a person, anyway. She only knew her as a mother-in-law and grandmother. But then she remembered the question Chloe had asked her, 'what do you like doing, Granny?' She remembered how shocked she'd felt that she'd been unable to joyfully answer, unable even to identify what she liked doing.

"You can be quite inscrutable, you know," she said seriously, accepting the glass Giselle offered. "I was feeling rattled that you thought you knew something about me that I didn't realise myself and then I remembered how Chloe had nudged me into doing something I liked, the watercolour classes, and now I love it. So what might you nudge me into?"

Giselle smiled. "Well since you're being candid so will I, but only as candid as I think is good for you," she said solemnly.

"I'm not a child, Giselle."

"I know that. And yet sometimes people, whatever their age, need someone to care for them and look after them and sometimes advice can be helpful, or if not advice, just a caring observation." Giselle curled up in her chair again and sipped her wine. The silence between them lengthened. Alison felt the warmth of the fire and, smiling, accepted the warmth of Giselle's affection. She waited for her to speak again.

"When you've been terribly hurt, often all your energy is just taken up with surviving each day and there's nothing of you left to do anything but survive. Struggling to survive is a tough call. And I can see that for your generation doing what you're doing right now is even harder than it is for mine."

"And why is that?" Alison shot back at her.

Giselle was unflinching. "You guys sort of moved into your husband's world. You literally gave up your own world and moved to James'. And now you haven't got a world to move back to and you have to create one. I can see that. Look at it. Why are you here tonight? You're helping me out; helping me to do what I want to do. When I married Ed, I kept my world. When I had the children, I kept my world. And now, thanks to you, now and at the other times you've come running, I can keep my world and I love it. I love the design world, love doing what I'm good at and I love the appreciation of a job well done. But I can see how hard it must be for you not having a world to go back to, especially after all those years abroad. You'd hardly started your own career when you married James and you then embarked on supporting his career. That's over. So what have you got now? You've got us and Nick, of course, and your sisters and friends…"

Alison felt the tears sliding down her face and she closed her eyes and let them slide. She heard Giselle put down her glass and felt her sit on the sofa beside her, felt her limp hand enclosed in Giselle's hand, felt Giselle offer a tissue. Sitting up, she blew her nose. Giselle handed over the box of tissues.

"It's OK, Alison. It's good to cry."

"I'd really rather not cry, you know. I'm supposed to be here to help you, not collapsing in a weeping heap."

"But that's just what I'm saying. This is a two-way street, you know. We help each other. I didn't mean to upset you and I think probably you needed just to let that out. You'll feel better now."

Alison sniffed and blew and got up and threw the tissues on the fire. "You're right, Giselle. It has felt like survival at times and I have been aware that I must make my own world. You and Ed and Nick are so supportive but you do have your own lives to lead and I don't really want to need supporting." She laughed ruefully.

"And how do you feel you've done so far, making your own world?" Giselle asked with a smile.

"Pretty damn good if you want an honest answer. I like my house. I like my garden and I like the challenge of the painting and this exhibition coming up."

"Well, I for one am full of admiration, Alison. I think you've done fantastically. So what happens now?"

"Well…I told you. The painting and the exhibition."

"The only good thing about James doing what he did was leaving you secure financially, wouldn't you say?"

"Giselle, there was nothing good about what James did. Nothing. Can I help myself to another glass of wine?"

"Of course. Listen, what I was trying to say was I know you must feel fortunate that at least financially you have no major worries. But you're not the sort of person who can sit back and feel grateful, are you? It's not enough, is it? And if I'm being candid, Alison, I don't imagine you're in a hurry to embrace another relationship, are you?"

"Now that is the truth." Alison was vehement. She stood up and paced back and forth in front of the fire. "Nothing could be further from my mind. But you're right about me doing something. Clearly I'm not in a position to start a career…"

"I don't see why not."

"You don't?" Alison stopped pacing and turned and looked at Giselle. "But what about my age?"

"I don't think age comes into it. I think you can do what you want. You could start to train for something entirely new, take a degree course, open a shop, start up a business, anything."

Alison laughed, a delighted, liberated peal of laughter, and sank back onto the sofa. "Giselle, you're a darling. I could, could I? Well there is something required and that is the drive, the incentive, the passion to do it. And the energy of course."

"And what do you have the drive and energy for?"

"Darling girl. As it happens, I am literally on the verge of finding out."

A door banged. Keys clattered into a bowl and the hall cupboard opened and shut.

"Hi Ed," Giselle called. "We're in here." Alison was walking to the door to meet him, gave him a warm hug and released him to go and kiss his wife.

"You're just in time to hear your mother pronounce," said Giselle. "Can he hear, Alison? We're talking passion and energy, Ed."

Alison looked at them. How on earth did she get into this position? Here she was, standing in front of her son and daughter-in-law talking about herself and she was going to show off. To hell with it, that's what she would do.

"For your benefit, Ed, very briefly, it was Giselle who started this whole thing, this conversation, and now I'll finish it.

I want to support a charity called Cleanwater, in a big and committed way, and I can see a way of doing it using my new-found joy in watercolour painting. Oh, and I've started by painting my garden. And my painting teacher is very encouraging and thinks I've got something." She stood, hands behind her back, finished, complete. "He really was very, very encouraging." She smiled happily. "I was so pleased I couldn't stop thinking about it for days. I know exactly what you mean, Giselle, when you say how nice it is for your efforts to be appreciated." Giselle applauded, whilst Ed looked bemused. Giselle laughed and hugged him and Alison laughed and hugged him.

"What have you two been drinking?" he asked.

"A lovely light Chenin Semillon," said Giselle. "Let's have supper and you can have some too."

As THEY SAT at the kitchen table, the phone rang. Ed reached for it.

"Hello. Ed Henderson. Nick! Hi there. Yes, Mum's here. No, no, everything's fine. The kids have got chickenpox and Giselle's tied up with work tomorrow and the next day so Mum's helping out. Yes of course. Here she is." He passed the phone to Alison.

"Darling," she said, "I'm so sorry. I was going to text you but what with one thing and another I didn't. Huge apologies. It was very kind of you to send me a message via Kellie-Ann." She raised her eyebrows and gave a 'what is all this about?' shrug of the shoulders to Ed. "I'll be back by Friday. Lovely. 'Bye." She handed the phone to Ed.

"I really don't know what that was about. Nick has been coming and going in a completely ad hoc way and now suddenly he's telling me his movements and even when his plans change, which he's never done before. And he's never wondered where I might be. Something is afoot."

Ed laughed. "What a suspicious mind you have, Mum."

"Not suspicious. Experienced and intuitive. Anyway, it's very sweet of him to be concerned about me. Now, since I'm on a roll, would you like to hear all about this exhibition and, even more importantly, Cleanwater?"

16

It was with a smile that Alison unlocked her front door. So nice to be home again; and yes, it truly did feel like home.

She ran up the stairs and unpacked the few things from her overnight bag, putting it away in the cupboard on the landing with a satisfied shove. It had been lovely to see the children and she was glad they were recovering, but how nice it was to pick up the threads of her own life. She checked the answerphone. Five messages. Four were a brief silence followed by a cut-off click and an abrupt one from Aidan. The exhibition. Please call. She did so immediately and at Aidan's insistence agreed to a meeting in the morning.

"I'VE MISSED YOU, MY FRIEND," he said, taking her hand and kissing her swiftly on the cheek. "Come in and have coffee. We've a lot to get galvanised."

"Galvanised? That sounds far too energetic a word for you, Aidan."

"Well, someone has to do the galvanising and get this show on the road because so far all we've got are some prospective dates and a lot of intentions. And you, my friend," he poured aromatic coffee from a battered enamel pot and handed her a mug, "have dwelt entirely on the possible proceeds to your charity with no thought paid to the actual exhibition." He sat down and looked at her, unsmiling.

"Just a minute, are you criticising me?"

"Yes."

"Well, perhaps you'd tell me why." Alison banged her mug onto the table in front of her.

"You may well look at me in that indignant way and I hope I've ruffled your feathers enough to galvanise you into action. You agreed to do this with me; in fact you were very enthusiastic. Perhaps you'd tell me exactly what you've put in place." He draped himself over his chair in his inimitable way, but his eyes never left her face. Alison opened her mouth a couple of times, closing it, wordless; gestured with a hand, cleared her throat. The silence lengthened. Aidan drank his coffee. Alison folded her arms on the table in front of her. She took a deep breath.

"OK, Aidan. You are clearly asking me to account for myself. Well, it seems we do have a celebrity who's agreed to be involved."

"Oh joy."

"Well, it's a start, isn't it? And I've been working hard at the paintings I intend to exhibit."

"Alison, you clearly have no idea what's involved to make a good job of this. Your efforts thus far, and do feel free to correct me if I'm wrong, have been all about you. YOU had this somewhat holier than thou charity idea. YOU'VE been doing YOUR painting and YOU'VE been seeking a celebrity of YOUR choice to publicise YOUR charity. You gave me the impression that you had some experience in organising events such as these when you were drifting about the world at the expense of the British taxpayer. Well you may be my much loved friend, but I'm hugely unimpressed thus far."

"There's no need to be rude." Alison looked at him indignantly

"Rudeness be buggered. I've told you the truth. Haven't I?" His voice was mild and his look was steady as he waited for an answer. She had to be honest and she felt angry with herself. He was right and it was all David's fault. If only the wretched man had done what she'd wanted and refused to be associated with this! She shook her head and straightened up, bracing herself with honesty.

"Aidan, I'm sorry. You're right. I've been hugely focussed on myself for a long time now and I can see it's time to move on. Thank you." She smiled. "You really are my friend and I appreciate your galvanising nudge."

"Oh bloody hell, Alison, what a truly nice person you are."

"Well clearly not, since I've been so self-centred, but I do accept what you say and I'm ready to hear what we need to do."

"Alison, you're supposed to be organising this. I'm the artist, remember? I'm sorting the paintings, the painters, the hanging and the emotional support, and believe me it'll be required. By the painters. The deal is that you, my dear friend, will do the rest."

"OK. Well, I'll fix the dates and the publicity."

"I know you say you've organised charity events, Alison, but have you specifically organised an art exhibition?"

"No."

"Right. Well I'm not the best organised person in the world myself, but I've had a chat with the guy who runs the gallery that takes some of my stuff and in order to do this really well, and I assume that you think, like me, unless it's going to be done really well there's no point in doing it at all, there are things that you must consider. For instance, the exhibition space, allowing time for promotional material, a mailing list, local radio and press, list of invitees…"

Alison had her hand up. "All of that I have ready to go. I will find a good angle for the local press, hence the celebrity opening and the charity connection and all of that. I honestly do know how to do all that. I have the contacts for local press, radio and TV, and some reporters to brief beforehand and to invite to the opening."

"Good. Now what about artists' statements?"

"What are they? And wouldn't that be up to you? As would the actual hanging of the pictures."

"Ah, yes, maybe, but you'll have to use some of the statements in the promotional stuff and you'll also have to take care of any practical problems with the hanging."

"Such as?"

"Well, some pictures need a light background like a white-washed wall, and plenty of space round them and some, the smaller ones, need a more intimate feel to put you closer to the image." Aidan ran his fingers distractedly through his hair.

"Aidan, I'm really sorry I knocked your confidence in me. I can see you're worried about this and you needn't be. We'll work as a team. It'll be fine. I just have to accept that I can't do anything about David Rowbottom. He's not my choice but we're stuck with him. I will make every effort to work with him and do this really well. You see," she stood up and raised a victory clenched fist, "you've galvanised me."

Aidan smiled with relief. "Thank goodness for that."

"We'll do an action list together, who does what, and tick it off as we go. No Ts uncrossed, no Is undotted. What would you like me to put at the top of the list?"

"Get everyone together so I can see who's intending to exhibit what. I've already decided about my own material."

"Right. I'll do the phoning. Village Hall next painting afternoon suit you? That'll be Monday. Two days' time."

.   .   .

ALISON BRACED herself as the first of Aidan's students pushed through the doors of the hall carrying a large portfolio and what looked like framed pictures wrapped in an old curtain. Her own pictures, all unframed as yet, were neatly laid on a table waiting for Aidan to look at them.

"Hello Henry," she smiled in welcome, "could you take yours up to the front please? I'm just going to allocate spaces as people arrive."

A rush of air as the door swung open and more voices followed and suddenly everyone seemed to arrive at once. Gradually Alison had all the tables taken and anticipation built as they waited for Aidan to assess the pictures. He stood on the stage at the end of the hall and clapped for silence.

"Good afternoon everyone. It's really good to see you all and to see how much you've brought with you, so thank you for your hard work. Now, there are some ground rules I think we must first agree. Will you let me be the final judge about what goes into the exhibition and where it's hung, no argument? You'll have to trust me to display everyone's work in the best way I can." People looked at one another and shuffled and some nodded. "I'd like a show of hands please. Do you agree?" The show of hands was unanimous. "Good. I'm going to assess all your work this afternoon and while I'm doing this, you must each write for me what's called an artist's statement. Alison will give you pens and paper for this." Appreciative looks were exchanged and smiles hovered. This was professional stuff. "An artist's statement gives the viewer of your pictures a glimpse into who you are as a person. People like to know about you and it gives them an opportunity to understand through the written word as well as your paintings and offers them a chance to connect with you." He paused and his words sank into the silence. "Now, the other thing you need to be aware of is that an exhibition represents years of hard work, investment in time and money and tremendous emotional commitment. I'm sure you'd all agree with that. You will have expectations, as will the viewers, and sometimes you may be surprised at your own emotional response to this. You know how you, personally, like to be perceived by the world and in letting the world see your pictures and have your personal statement, you lose a certain amount of control of that perception. I promise my total support, my personal and confidential support, to each one of you if you need it. But," he held wide both his arms, "this is going to be exciting and the most enormous fun, so let's get started," and he jumped down from the stage and headed for the first collection of pictures.

ALISON ARRIVED home exhausted but satisfied. She unloaded her car and carefully stashed her portfolio of pictures in the hall. They'd made good progress and Adrian felt the quality of the pictures was well up to the standard he'd hoped for. She kicked off her shoes, wriggled her toes gratefully and walked into her kitchen, enjoying the cool tiles under her bare feet. She glanced at her watch. Five o'clock. Time for a cup of tea and then a hot bath beckoned. The kettle was whistling when the front door opened.

"Hi Mum," Nick hustled Kellie-Ann before him into the kitchen.

"Hi," Alison poured the water into the teapot, "nice to see you both. Cup of tea?" She looked at them enquiringly. They stood side by side in front of her, holding hands, eyes wide, watching her, motionless. Silence gathered, fragmented by the sound of the mugs as she put them on the tea tray, the ting of a spoon, the sigh of the fridge door shutting when she'd finished filling the milk jug. No one spoke. Alison picked up the tray and moved towards them. They parted to let her through and followed her to the living room. She poured the tea, took a mug and subsided into a chair.

"Help yourselves." They did and still stood, watching her. "Well? Aren't you going to sit down?" She heard the irritable edge to her voice. What was the matter with them both? Nick looked anxious, hair dishevelled, his polo shirt with its Pentarron logo creased and spotted with oil, his jeans bagging at the knees. Kellie-Ann stood up straight, feet together, shiny hair drawn into a ponytail with a fluorescent purple band, orange fringe sharp edged across her forehead. Her bright pink hooped earrings matched her lipstick perfectly and her hands with hot-pink nails clasped the mug as she sipped her tea. The ponytail swung as she tossed her head and the earrings bobbed and twisted.

It was Kellie-Ann who broke the silence. "You OK Alison? You look tired."

"I am tired. I'm having this tea and then I'm going to sink into a hot bath. What are you two going to do?"

They looked at each other and turned back to Alison.

"Oh for heaven's sake!" She pushed herself up out of the chair. "Ever since you arrived the pair of you have stood there speechless and twitching. You've clearly got something to say, so either say it or it'll have to wait 'til after this bath of mine."

"Go on babe," Kellie-Ann nudged Nick.

"Kellie-Ann's got something to say." He turned to his beloved and said softly, "It'll be much better coming from you." The ponytail twitched and the earrings danced and Kellie-Ann shrugged.

"OK. Well, you know David Rowbottom..."

Alison's eyes narrowed and she stiffened. "I wouldn't say I know Mr Rowbottom, Kellie-Ann. I have met him, as you know, and attempted to be helpful to him but you probably also know that we didn't hit it off at all. And that's putting it mildly."

Kellie-Ann looked at Nick and then back to Alison again. "Well, there's lots of us who've been involved with his recovery and to tell the honest truth it's been very, very hard for him, but he's a fighter and he's put in the hours and put in the effort and..." her voice failed as she noticed the stony expression on Alison's face. "Did you have any messages on your answer-phone?" she asked in a smaller voice.

"I had four messages which were the sound of a phone being cut off. Could that be what you mean?"

Kellie-Ann looked uncertainly at Nick, who smiled encouragingly.

"Mum, please let her finish. This is important."

Alison folded her arms. Kellie-Ann's earrings danced and bobbed frenetically as she gathered herself and said in a rush, "David says you asked if he'd like to see your paintings and he says he would."

Nick slipped his arm round Kellie-Ann's waist. "And here they are." Smiling, he indicated the paintings stacked against the wall. Alison was speechless. She certainly had not invited him. He'd asked to be invited but she had never issued the invitation. "So your bath will have to wait, Mum, because David will be here in five. OK babe?" He looked lovingly at Kellie-Ann, took his car keys out of his pocket, grabbed her hand and headed for the door.

"Now just a minute," Alison ran a hand distractedly through her hair, "what exactly are you saying?"

Kellie-Ann paused in her flight. "You won't regret this, Alison. If you knew how down David has been and how hard the struggle was..."

"I know nothing about David Rowbottom's struggle," said Alison with rising fury, "and you may remember, Kellie-Ann, that both you and your mother slapped confidentiality all over the place if I so much as asked a question about him and to be perfectly frank I now have no wish to know anything nor to meet him nor, indeed, to show him my pictures." She trailed off limply; tired, confused, untidy and wordless.

Nick gave Kellie-Ann a tug through the arched doors and they crossed the garden, leaving the garden door open.

Alison heard a car door shut and in the gathering dusk she saw David Rowbottom manoeuvre his wheelchair through the garden door, pushing it shut behind him. She watched as he paused, seeming to gather himself and then, powerful hands on the black steel rims of the wheels, he slowly pushed himself along the path, looking to left and right, pausing at the roundel where the green of the herbs was pushing through the dark earth then looking, was it with apprehension, towards the lighted windows of The Stables. Alison almost laughed. What a situation. What was she to do? Should she rush outside with a cry? "Stay right where you are, you obnoxious man. Turn round and return whence you came!" Of course not. She had no choice but to go through with this ridiculous charade. She opened the heavy glass door and deliberately put out of her mind the thought that her hair was a mess, her makeup long gone and her feet bare.

17

With carefully arranged nonchalance, Alison leant against the doorframe, arms folded. David had paused and turned his back on the house, manoeuvring his wheelchair under the little tree, taking in his surroundings. She observed him minutely, this enigma of a man who so disconcertingly came in and out of her life with such awkwardness and such inconvenience. She took in the crisp pale blue collar at the round neck of his dark sweater, the jeans and the pristine trainers which rested on the footplates of his wheelchair. Did he know she was standing in the doorway? She wondered if at any moment he might retreat; might indeed go back across the garden, back 'whence he came'. But no, with a movement of one hand he turned the wheelchair and saw her, raised a hand in greeting and came towards her.

"Hello there," he said affably.

"Hi." She straightened up.

"It's good of you to show me your paintings." He looked relaxed, head tilted to look at her, the slightest of smiles lifting the corners of his mouth, reaching his clear eyes, warming his cool direct gaze. A breeze ruffled his dark hair and the tiny new leaves of the little tree shivered. She heard the clinking chink of her bird feeders as they gently collided in its moving branches.

"Well, 'show' is probably not the right word," she said, "but Nick and Kellie-Ann said you were coming to have a look at them." She hoped her gaze was as cool as his, but no smile reached her eyes. Silence grew. She resisted the urge to speak again. He raised an eyebrow. She remained motionless, hands in her pockets, bare feet firm on the smooth tiles, jaw getting stiff as she clenched her teeth. He leaned back in the wheelchair, his hands resting lightly on the wheel rims.

"So, if you're not prepared to show me your paintings, how would you like me to," he paused, "look at your paintings? I think we might insert the word 'see' here, too, don't you? I came to 'see' your paintings. Since you asked me to open your exhibition I thought it would be useful to 'see'", he paused for emphasis, "what my opening was going to 'show'", another pause, "to the unsuspecting public. However," his smile broadened, "I'm very happy to continue looking at you." Alison felt the familiar irritation surge through her and with exasperation she pulled her hands from her pockets and placed them on her hips. As she drew breath to speak, David said, "Oh, such adversarial body language! I come in peace. Honestly. I'm here just to look, even glance, at your paintings. How about a glance? A swift one?" His voice was gentle, reasonable. His whole demeanour was calm and courteous.

Whatever is the matter with me, thought Alison. Why don't I just get on with this and then I can have my hot bath and my cold wine. She moved aside in the doorway and with a tight smile said, "Will you fit, I mean with the chair? Is the doorway wide enough?"

"Oh yes. Kellie-Ann was good enough to measure it." He wheeled his way into the room and stopped the chair, turning it expertly to face her.

"My paintings are over here," Alison said. "I've just brought them back from the Village Hall. Aidan was assessing them this afternoon."

"Quite a few," said David. "D'you want a hand moving them when you have to do it again? We could do it in one trip in my car."

"That won't be necessary. I mean, I'm sorted, thank you. Anyway, perhaps you'd better have your glance now." She stopped talking abruptly. "I'll pull the pictures out one by one. Will you position yourself where you can best see them?"

"Fine. I'll sit in that chair, shall I?"

Alison looked at him with surprise. He was sitting in his wheelchair. Why would he want another chair?

The smile and affability was gone from his face. Reaching behind him, he pulled what looked like folded metal rods from the back of his chair and his strong hands deftly manipulated and clicked the rods into a frame in front of him. Alison saw a small twitch at the side of his jaw as he pushed himself up from the chair, transferred his hands to the frame and stood in front of her. He looked down at her and her backward step was uncertain as she took in his surprising height.

The last of the pale light from the garden glanced off the metal that surrounded him, the rods of the walking frame, spokes and rims of wheels, the heavy aviator's watch on his wrist, hands white knuckled as he gripped the frame. Suddenly she saw through the visible support that held him upright, enabled his mobility, affirmed his independence. She sensed his power and determination and at the same time felt the poignancy of his situation. Amidst all that support, the technology, the amazing super-light, super-strong metal; the stunningly clever design; the expertise that had taught him how to do this, it was the aviator's watch which caught her. He was a flyer. He should be soaring high above this small place, this tiny piece of England where she had sought refuge. How strange that they were momentarily together in these old stables, she finding security and wrapping herself in familiarity and routine; he forced to be here, grounded, his wings clipped, his heroic efforts reduced to miniscule signs of progress as he valiantly battled his disability.

"That chair'll do," and slowly, deliberately, he walked the steps required, turned and sat. Alison was speechless. He grinned at her, and she could see his suppressed delight at his achievement. "You're smiling," he said.

"Am I?" She felt foolish again.

"You are, and it suits you. I haven't often seen you smile."

"You haven't often given me reason to smile!"

"I haven't recently had reason to smile myself."

Alison hesitated, unprepared for his sudden vulnerability, shaken by her own emotional response.

"Oh come on. You've got everything! You're a successful man! You've had your creativity recognised and you're a big-name writer. You've got plenty of reason to smile," she said robustly.

"You're a hard woman, Mrs H." He shifted his position in the chair as he smiled broadly at her. "One day I'll tell you what I haven't got. But now, on with the glance."

"Oh very clever." She acknowledged his play on words. "But of course you are a writer. Though I have to tell you I'm not a fan of your books." She sat down opposite him.

"Well there's a surprise. You're quite clearly not a fan of anything to do with me. So you've tried my books?"

"Not actually read one, but had a look. In a bookshop. No. That's not quite true. I did buy one but, well, to be perfectly honest the whole subject matter is abhorrent to me; violence, aggression, glorifying war, that sort of thing."

"Wow. What a sweeping generalisation that is. So how come you want me, this purveyor of abhorrent nastiness, to be associated with your squeaky clean charity?"

"Now you ask, I didn't want you to do it. You were not my idea. You were the committee's idea. Being local, I suppose. Local hero I think was the term used. I had never heard of you and you would not have been my choice."

"How very frank of you. So you don't buy into that hero stuff?"

"How could I? I know nothing about you."

"But when you looked at the book you bought, could you not see any moral content, any good overcoming evil, courage in the face of impossible odds, heroic selflessness? I'm not talking about me, you understand, but about people I've known and things I've seen." His voice was hard-edged and his eyes cold as he sat back in the chair, his hands balled into fists. He was breathing deeply and she could see he was reigning in his feelings, rearranging his expression, retrieving his sardonic mask.

"I didn't read the book. I saw the images on the cover, and read the blurb on the back and dipped into it and it just isn't my sort of subject." She felt the silence become a yawning chasm between them. "Perhaps you'd rather not do this after all?" she said, surprised at the ambivalence she felt as she asked the question. "No, wait. See the paintings first."

She got up and began to shift the paintings. "I think if I just move them from this side to over there you could have your glance and they'd still be neatly stacked." She busied herself with her organising and he watched silently as she knelt to make a final adjustment.

"Alison." His powerful voice was low and he spoke her name with such gentleness that she turned awkwardly on her knees to look at him. "You'll never know how much I'd like to come over there and move those paintings for you." She sat back on her heels. He smiled ruefully and made a deprecating movement with his hands. She felt her mouth curve into an answering smile and her body subsided as she let out a long gentle breath, followed by a slow, deep breath in. The tower clock struck eight and neither moved.

Suddenly Alison's face contorted with pain. Her legs were stiffening under her. Damn. Awkwardly she got to her feet, grunting unattractively as she did so. The deeply peaceful feeling vanished as her mood turned to guilt that she had been so unkind to someone who she could see was clearly making great efforts to deal with his situation. Get a grip, she told herself, confused. She suddenly felt like a schoolgirl whose behaviour had been found wanting.

"Thank you," she said hurriedly, stretching one leg and then the other, "That's nice of you. It would be lovely to have your help, but I can manage. Really. They're not heavy."

David said nothing as she showed him her paintings. She felt him watching her but studiously avoided returning his look. In silence she passed them in front of him, restacking them against the wall; pictures of her garden, studies of shadows and dappled light, the tree with its fattening buds, the clock tower glistening in the rain, a still life of an old trowel with a ragged glove. She heard him breathe, sensed his presence, breathed the crisp, fresh scent of him. She was acutely aware of his powerful frame, sitting forward in the chair, studying the pictures intently. How extraordinary it had been to see him standing; to see him walking. And yet how painful his grip on the walking frame; the effort of his steps. When the last picture was neatly stacked she looked at him; waited for him to speak.

"Well...I think we can inflict your paintings on the unsuspecting public."

"You can imagine what a relief that is to me," she said with irony.

"I like your paintings."

"Oh good."

"Well, obviously agreeing to open your exhibition doesn't give me any control over what goes into it..."

"No it certainly doesn't. Aidan has the control."

"Ah yes. The magnificent and creative Aidan. I'm told his faithful flock hang onto his every word."

"You speak as though we're sheep! He's a good tutor and I for one have found his support and encouragement invaluable."

"Have you now?" David's look darkened. "And how has he been supporting you?"

"I don't think that's really any of your business. Aidan is an excellent tutor and has been a good friend to me at times..." her voice trailed away. She made another attempt, "...at times when I've found life difficult."

"I know you've had a tough time lately." The statement he made was matter-of-fact.

"I don't think that's anything to do with you," she flashed back at him, acutely aware of her ungraciousness.

"Ah Mrs H. There's the madam in you again. I know I can be prickly but you're something else!"

"I don't need a commentary on my character. I didn't ask you here. This was your idea, not mine."

"Well, as to the idea," he was leaning forward intently, "it seemed reasonable to me that since you asked me to open your exhibition, involved me for your own purposes, I should just have an idea of what sort of exhibition this was going to be. After all, my reputation as Hal Davidson is, and I'm being totally honest here, vital to me."

The meaning of his words penetrated Alison's emotional response and she felt the madam in her really rise up.

"What you're saying is you came here to get an idea of the quality of my paintings so you could judge whether or not this exhibition will be worthy to be opened by Hal Davidson?"

"Precisely. And before you do the outraged madam bit again, just think about that practically. Here am I, forced to find a way to make a living and yes, I've been fortunate with the writing, but part of the whole thing is the persona, you know? It doesn't just happen, a bestseller. There's all sorts of behind-the-scenes stuff which goes on to the extent that Hal Davidson is a piece of merchandise, promoted and sold time and again. And just in case writing is the only way I'll ever be able to earn a living, I have to be careful with him. I don't do celebrity stuff as a rule, and therefore I just needed to know what sort of outfit you were, you and...Aidan. Please," his look was weary, "do just think about what I'm saying. This is a business arrangement. I'm happy to help and I can see Cleanwater's a good cause and now I've seen your paintings I can tell you that yes, I will do the celebrity stuff your committee wants me to. Don't ask me why, but I will. Let's just say I like a challenge and if ever there was a challenge, working with you is it! Just tell me when and where you want me..." He left the sentence unfinished, an eyebrow raised. Alison shifted uncomfortably. David's smile was wide. What was so funny? Was he laughing at her? He was!

"I'll make sure you have all the information. And I suppose you'd like to see the publicity material before it goes out?"

"Now that is most courteous. So are you offering me a little control? Some editorial control perhaps?"

"Well, that seems only fair. I'll be using your name, after all. I take it it's OK to use Hal Davidson?"

"Sure."

"Great." Alison smiled. "Hang on. I'm just going to jot some things down. As you're here, we could have a meeting. Do you agree? But first, my cold glass of wine is well overdue. Will you have one?"

"D'you have a beer?"

"I think there's some of Nick's lager in the fridge. Nick is my son."

"I know. Kellie-Ann's boyfriend."

"Of course. How stupid of me."

She felt flustered again as she left the room; flustered and resigned both at the same time. I give up, she thought. She screwed the corkscrew into the cold bottle aggressively. "Well," she muttered under her breath, "he might as well stay for a beer as it doesn't seem as though he's going away. He seems to be planted. Taking root." She yanked the cork from the bottle.

"Who's taking root?"

"Nick! Where the hell did you spring from? I didn't hear the door."

"We came through the garden. Kellie-Ann and me." He took another can of lager from the fridge. "Isn't he fantastic, Mum? I mean, don't you think he's a great guy? After all he's been through? And now at last, this."

Alison held up her hand. "Say no more, Nick. Stop right there." She poured wine into a glass, put the bottle down, picked up the glass and drank. "I don't know what you mean by 'and now this'. In fact, I know nothing about David. I cannot judge him. I know nothing of his background except that he has been injured. I don't at all like the books with which he appears to earn his living. As you very well know I'm trying to get this event together to raise funds for a charity which is very close to my heart, and his high profile will be briefly useful for that event. That's it. Sum total. End of. Great and fantastic are not words I would use to describe him. No." She put up her hand again as Nick started to speak.

He grabbed it and said quietly, urgently, "Mum, his effort in being here tonight, alone and without help, being normal and walking, is immense. I am asking you to recognise that, at least. You may not be able to make a judgement about him but I can. And I think he's great."

He let go of her hand and took beers and glasses with him as he left the kitchen. Alison heard the voices, Kellie-Ann's excited and twittering; Nick's light and interested; David's calm, assured, deep with its sense of latent power. Alison sipped her wine. I give up, she thought. The man is thrust upon me. She giggled. Bad choice of word. Come along now. Let's have a bit of decorum, shall we? But she saw her reflection briefly as she walked through the hall in her bare feet. A tousled, untidy, frazzled-looking fiftysomething, she thought. Too bad. She tossed the hair from her face and glided into the living room.

"WELL, ISN'T THIS NICE," Alison knew her smile was brittle as she deliberately interrupted the conversation. "My paintings have apparently been accepted so we can go ahead with the exhibition. A lot of work to do and a lot of money to raise." Her smile radiated as she looked at David, then Nick, then Kellie-Ann. She sipped her wine and waited. This gathering in her living room was nothing to do with her. She hadn't arranged it, hadn't invited David Rowbottom or Nick and Kellie-Ann to be here. What happened next was not her responsibility. They could sit there talking all evening if they wished. She'd finish her wine and then go and have her bath. She smiled serenely. No one spoke. Kellie-Ann's hoops bobbed and jangled and she cleared her throat. She looked meaning-fully at Nick.

"OK babe?" she said, "time to go?"

Alison saw David begin to gather himself for the effort of standing and found herself shrinking from being present again to witness his struggle as he returned his reluctant body to the wheelchair. She got up.

"Well, Nick, I'll leave you to see everyone out, shall I?"

Kellie-Ann shot out of her chair and headed for the glass doors. "No, no," she said, opening the door, "come on Nick, I'll be late. Gotta go. Thanks Alison," and she was through the doors with Nick in hot pursuit, a "'Bye Mum," delivered over his shoulder.

"Looks like you're stuck with me," said David, reaching for his frame, "but don't worry. Have frame, will travel."

"I'm sorry. I didn't mean to rush everyone. It's just..."

"Just you're not comfortable with someone in a wheelchair?"

"Why must everything focus on you? No. What I'm feeling is nothing to do with you. I'm not unfamiliar with people who live with disability. I've lived in the Third World, helped charity workers, seen a lot, believe me. Why d'you think I want to do this fundraising? No, your wheelchair does not give me difficulty, but you do."

"I do? How can that possibly be? What difficulty have I ever given you?"

"I don't think it would be useful to recall your questionable manners and off-hand treatment when I came to your house to help."

"Possibly not. I was in a somewhat vulnerable position then. It was early days after my surgery and the risks were still great, which would reasonably account for my unaccustomed tension. I have no sympathy for wimps and found my situation hard to tolerate. Plus, if I'm honest, I found you insufferable."

"You found me insufferable. How dare you? All I did was come to help, to help Virginia, actually."

"There you were, always perfect, elegantly dressed and swanning about the village being plucky. You could do no wrong. In spite of your own difficulties and sadness, you pulled yourself up by your boot straps and tried to start again. And just when the going was really tough for me, you and your pluckiness came into my life. The day you arrived like Little Red Riding Hood I was feeling completely overwhelmed at my own inadequacy. The surgery was the last attempt and no one knew whether or not it would work."

"I know nothing about your problems. Why did you have to

have the surgery?" Alison ignored his opinion of her pluckiness.

"I ejected from a Tornado. Not to be recommended." His smile was rueful as he rubbed his leg. "Coming out of that plane I hit air at 650 knots and it was like hitting a brick wall. I was the commander and I ejected the guy with me too. He didn't make it." He looked bleakly at Alison. "I landed badly." Alison felt pierced by the pain on his face. He spoke again. "You can never be sure you did the right thing. Could I have landed safely? Should I have ejected sooner? Later?"

It was as though David had pulled back a curtain. She could see the torment he'd suffered; not just the struggle with his injuries as he tried to walk again, but the struggle within himself and his uncertainty. He spoke again.

"I don't know why I'm telling you all this. If there's one thing I can't stand it's pity; the pity of others or self-pity. I was in my element, flying. I know I was lucky and I had a great career. People thrive in their own element, don't they? When you're in your own element you're OK. Fish in the sea, birds in the air. I feel I'm searching for my element and I'll know when I've found it. I'll be able to breathe again."

His look was bleak. She knew what he meant. Here, she was in her element, in this building which was her home; in her garden which had kindled her nurturing instincts and gave her joy with its response and in this village, this small society where she had found new interests and new belonging. He was so out of place here; too big, too restless, too confined.

"Sometimes people never find their true element, but they can be content." Her voice was gentle.

"Content! Is that what you're striving for? Contentment?"

"We aren't talking about me. We're talking about you." Alison looked at him without a smile.

"Well, maybe we should be talking about you."

She shook her head. She was absolutely certain that she would not talk about herself.

"No. Tell me about the walking."

"Do you really want to know?"

"Do you think that I'm sitting here, exhausted after a long day and looking like the wreck of the Hesperus asking a question merely to make conversation? You can be so exasperating."

"I prefer your exasperation to your pity."

"You've never had pity from me. As I've already told you, I've seen people far worse off than you and without hope. If it's exasperation you want, I can give you plenty. So I repeat, tell me about the walking."

"I will confess to you, Madam, that being on my feet feels like a miracle. The challenge has been huge and to my shame there have been days when I have felt defeated and yelled, 'sod it, get out of here' to the physios. But people like Maggie and Kellie-Ann have refused to let me give in. I had to keep working on my upper-body strength and then do ankle exercises and practice standing and weight bearing and eventually started treadmill training and progressive ambulation. I have no idea how far I'll be able to go but I'll bloody well keep trying."

"And is the career truly over?"

"You mean flying? Oh yes. I'm past the age of being any use and flying a desk doesn't interest me. But I do the books. I still do that abhorrent violent stuff. And I do it well." His look was challenging. She took up the challenge.

"Well that's your choice, isn't it, to spend your time and energy churning out that sort of stuff. And I can see it gets you back in your element, in a way."

"Perhaps. But you don't seem to mind getting on my bandwagon when it suits you. It's because of the books you asked me to open the exhibition."

"I've already made it clear that you were the choice of the committee. As far as I'm concerned, you are at liberty to decline their invitation."

"Oh I don't think I'll decline. It's a really good cause, Cleanwater. Maybe if I help your fundraising you'll look more kindly on my literary efforts."

"My regard, whether kind or otherwise, has no importance. What is important is getting this job done."

"Of course. Very worthy. Total integrity. That's what we'll do."

"I'll get copies of the publicity to you. Just let me know if you want any changes made. Can I give you a hand at all, with your wheelchair or anything?"

"Ah, I'm dismissed, am I?"

"No, not dismissed. But it's the end of a long day, so please forgive me."

ALISON WATCHED AS DAVID STOOD, drew himself carefully to his full height and took the few, slow, deliberate steps to his chair and lowered himself into it, becoming the figure she was more familiar with. He snapped and clicked the frame and it was stowed away. With one hand, he spun the chair full circle and faced her.

"Right. Saddled up and ready to roll. Mrs Henderson," he gave a mock salute, "I do like your paintings. They're very revealing," and he wheeled himself towards the door. "I'll see myself out."

And he did. Alison watched as he disappeared into the gloom of the garden and heard the click of the garden gate. She didn't heave herself out of her chair and head for the longed-for bath until the sound of the Trailblazer had disappeared. And what, she thought, could my paintings possibly reveal to you, David Rowbottom? How could someone whose youth had been spent being a hot-shot flyer preparing for war detect anything from anyone's painting? And anyway, my paintings aren't about me, damn it! They're about the scene, the mood, the light. But in the back of her mind she remembered Aidan's insight of struggle, endurance and hope when he looked at her painting of the little tree. Oh no. She was not revealing herself to anyone. And certainly not to David Rowbottom.

18

The door swung shut behind her as Alison staggered into the Village Hall with the last of her paintings and placed them with the others. She was surprised she'd completed so many. And what an effort it had been at times. She remembered how she'd sit and take time to look at her subject, the shadows cast across damp flagstones or the light falling across the blue garden door, softening it in places and revealing its texture in others. She remembered how memories of James would creep in and loneliness would steal over her like mist rising from a valley. He was still so familiar to her; real, in a way, as someone is when they've been such an essential part of your life for so long. She wondered if he ever thought of her. Well, even if you came back now, James, it wouldn't be the same me you'd find. I'm much more selfish with far less give in me, so there wouldn't be room in my life for you. Or anyone, she thought. She felt an arm round her shoulder and a light kiss on the top of her head.

"Morning," said Aidan. She smiled. It was good to see him. She felt refreshed and ready to go.

"Hi there. So, boss, let's have your orders and we can get this show on the road."

"Coffee," said Aidan. "Let's go in the kitchen and we'll talk strategy."

Aidan talked about how they would use the space, taking into account the sizes of the different paintings and letting each one have the space to breathe without distraction but making sure there was an intimate feel, especially with the smaller pieces, to bring the viewer close to the painting. The flow of the people viewing had to be directed, he said, and the way the light fell was important. He produced a measuring tape, a plumb line and a spirit level.

"I'm determined we should do this as well as we possibly can," he said, "and I've got a couple of guys to come and give me a hand. Now, what about the publicity, Ali? How's it going?"

Alison pulled out her neatly typed sheets of A4 and outlined where she'd already sent flyers and leaflets and posters and where she would be putting up more. He liked her design, incorporating Cleanwater and the Village Hall with Hal Davidson's name prominently displayed.

"Does his name have to be so big?" asked Aidan.

"Of course. He's the celeb, the Name. We want people to come because of him."

"We want them to come to buy paintings."

"Well of course, but come on, Aidan, anything we can do to draw people in is valuable, don't you think? I'm going to Fordingham today to do a local radio interview, too. I'll tell them about the very elegant gala evening we're going to have and I'll make sure all the galleries are aware too, including the London ones. Who knows, there may be a hidden talent about to be discovered."

"Well, you seem to have everything covered."

"I hope so. I've left my paintings over there for you. I don't expect you to use them all, of course. I know you've got plenty. And the final thing we'll have to do is the price tags. I've ordered wrapping stuff to be delivered for all the sales we'll make. This is wonderful, Aidan. It's going to be such a success." She hugged him impulsively, then grabbed her bag and headed for her car.

TRAFFIC HAD ALREADY BUILT as she reached the edge of Fordingham and she could feel her stress levels rise. She should have allowed more time. What if she couldn't park? Oh get a grip, she said to herself. You've done this before; radio interviews in Cambodia and Tanzania and even Washington. Yes, but I didn't have to drive myself then and negotiate all this traffic and find somewhere to park.

At the radio station, Alison took a few deep breaths, straightened her simple berry coloured jersey skirt and undid the shiny buttons of her cropped ribbed cardigan. She fingered her pearl necklace. Did she look a bit 'mumsy'; shirt collar too neat; shoes too sensible and shiny? She'd prefer to be regarded as arty. Maybe she should have worn jeans and boots and a great jacket.

"Mrs Henderson?" A thin girl, all arms and legs, her expression harassed and dressed entirely in black, appeared. "Would you like to come with me, please?" She was led to the studio where the afternoon presenter greeted her; Shannon Greenburg, local radio diva with ambitions to broadcast to the nation. She was a large person with immaculate hair, a lovely complexion and perfectly manicured nails painted a shiny plum. The folds of her bright animal-print jacket engulfed her bulk as she overflowed her studio chair and her desk was covered with the detritus of her day – post-it notes, A4 pads, pens, piles of paper, mug, diary, tissues, a lipstick. Her voice was deep and plummy. She oozed confidence and was clearly in charge.

"Good afternoon Mrs Henderson," she said, not prising herself out of her chair. "Please do sit. Thank you, Melissa." She waved away the harassed girl.

"Thank you for the publicity information you sent us. But I know even more about you than you've told us. You've lived all over the world, haven't you, while you were in the diplomatic service? Was that how you became interested in Cleanwater?"

"Actually it was my ex-husband, not me, who was in the diplomatic service and I would rather not mention that, or him. I was hoping we could talk about the talents of these local artists and how we're raising money for Cleanwater. I wasn't really prepared to talk about me."

"Oh but that would be such a pity. You've led such an interesting life. And you must have some wonderful stories to tell," gushed Shannon.

"I'm sorry. I hope you won't feel I contacted you under false pretences and I don't know where you got the information about my time overseas, but I would rather not talk about myself, except as one of the local artists."

The presenter smiled a tight little smile. "The information is on the internet. I googled you, Mrs Henderson. Normal research prior to an interview."

Alison began to dislike the woman. Just as she was sure she did not reveal herself in her paintings, she wasn't equally sure she wouldn't reveal anything about herself on the radio.

"I see. And did you google Cleanwater too?"

"Naturally."

"Well, I trust you found enough information there for your interview. I can tell you about the joys of watercolour painting, and, of course, the gifts of our tutor, Aidan Forester. Plus the delightful community where I'm lucky enough to be living; a community which readily responds and draws together to help those in need." She held her ground and looked steadily at the interviewer. "I'm afraid I have to add that any questions about my previous life or my ex-husband I shall have to respond to with silence." She smiled sweetly in the face of Shannon Greenburg's irritated glare.

"I understand. Have you been interviewed on the radio before, Mrs Henderson?"

"Yes. But not in this country."

"Right. Well it's all pretty straightforward." The plummy voice became condescending. "Now, if you can avoid too many facts and figures while you talk to us I'd be grateful and just watch out for ums or ahs. This is a live broadcast."

"So exciting," murmured Alison.

"What would you say your key message is, Mrs Henderson? What is it you're hoping to put across? This is our community slot, you know."

"I'd like people to know we're having this fundraising event and for them to be interested and therefore come along to it. And also to raise the profile of Cleanwater. What would you say your key objective is?"

"I'm supposed to help you to promote your event, Mrs Henderson."

"Oh good." Alison smiled again.

The plummy presenter did not smile. "We have another interviewee joining us in just a moment. Ah yes, here he is. Hello Mr Davidson." This time she did prise herself out of her chair and advanced on David Rowbottom as he manoeuvred his wheelchair through the door. She bent to greet him, revealing alarming acres of bosom before reinserting herself in her chair. "Mr Davidson, do you know Alison Henderson? But of course, you must do. You're part of this wonderful community, are you not, where people rally round and help the needy."

"Good afternoon, Mrs Henderson." David smiled at Alison.

"Hello. I wasn't expecting to see you here."

"Weren't you? I thought you'd arranged this."

"We arranged it," the plummy voice intervened. "You are part of this enterprise, are you not, Mr Davidson, and as a much admired and rather hard-to-locate local celebrity," she smiled archly at him, "we were delighted you agreed to come."

David was unsmiling. He raised a questioning eyebrow at Alison, who shrugged and shook her head.

The plummy voice became plummier as David and Alison were introduced to the listening public.

"...and Hal Davidson, real-life hero, action man and writer of bestsellers. Now Mr Davidson, Hal, do tell us about this happening in Highvale." There was silence while David looked at Alison, winked and turned to Shannon Greenburg.

"I think Mrs Henderson is better equipped to answer that. I have a very small role."

Shannon turned reluctantly to Alison, who calmly gave the details of the exhibition, the venue and the times and dates.

"We're hoping to raise some really useful funds for a charity called Cleanwater..."

"Thank you Alison," interrupted Shannon Greenburg. She turned once again to David, presenting Alison with the vastness of her leopard-print back, "and what will your role be in this venture, Hal?" She smiled ingratiatingly. "Somewhat of a departure for you, is it not? I hear you only ever appear in public for signings of your books. Or perhaps you'll be promoting your latest book too?"

David began to drum his fingers irritably on the arm of his chair. "Mrs Henderson has just given you the details of this venture and its purpose. We are raising money for Cleanwater. Do you know how important clean water is, Ms Greenburg? And do you know how many people don't have clean water and how many children die daily as a result? Tell her, Alison."

Alison was astonished at the impact she felt on his use of her first name. "Tell her," he commanded as she continued to gaze at the leopard-skin back. She cleared her throat and with quiet conviction, she explained.

"Every day in Africa alone 2,000 children die as a result of dirty water. There is a crisis in the world which can be resolved with safe water. Here, you and I turn on a tap without threatening our babies and children. We just take it for granted. Clean water underpins health by going to the very heart of communities and transforming people's lives."

Shannon Greenburg had turned to face her and Alison could see David smiling and nodding. Shannon spoke again, a hard edge cutting through the fruitiness of her voice. "And you've been to these countries, haven't you Alison? You've seen at firsthand the deprivation of parts of the Third World. Would you tell us about it? Would you tell us how you felt, when you were living such a high-profile glamorous life, a life financed by the British taxpayer, how it felt to witness this crisis?"

Alison stiffened. Shannon, sleek and cat-like, was poised as she waited for Alison's answer.

"Oh Ms Greenburg," David's voice sounded amused, "you won't get Mrs Henderson to talk about herself. Oh no. Believe me, I've tried and failed too. But," he smiled broadly, "if you ask her about watercolour painting, about the talented group who are going to be sharing their creativity with us in this exhibition, then I'm sure she'd answer. For me, personally, it will be an honour and a delight to open the exhibition and support Cleanwater and I'd like to publicly thank Mrs Henderson," he laughed in a chummy way as he allowed the full force of his smiling grey eyes to bathe Shannon Greenburg with conspiratorial good humour, "or to tell you the truth, I should thank her very discerning and enlightened committee whose choice I was, for giving me this opportunity. There is to be a wonderful opening, is there not, Mrs Henderson? Will you tell Ms Greenburg, Shannon, about it? I'm sure you're dying to hear, aren't you Shannon?" He smiled chummily again at Shannon. "Over to you, Mrs Henderson."

Alison, transfixed by his performance, suddenly realised she should speak quickly before Shannon extracted herself from the glow of David's chumminess.

"We are, of course, delighted that..." she hesitated. She'd never called him by his name. And what name was she to use? Quick. Any second now, Shannon would pounce again, "… that Hal Davidson is supporting us. The paintings are all by students of Aidan Forester who will also be exhibiting. He's a talented artist and a gifted tutor and you'll see wonderful results of the many hours of work and inspiration we've had as his pupils." She could see Shannon turn from David's gaze to face her and rushed on, "The exhibition will be opened with a gala evening at the Village Hall in High-vale. We'll have champagne and canapés and a very exciting raffle. If there's any one out there who would like to be part of this and donate more raffle prizes we'd be most grateful, as will Cleanwater. But do come and see our exhibition and enjoy the results of the creativity of these artists. It's a celebration of life and I hope will give many people pleasure. We all look forward to welcoming you to Highvale."

She sat back, triumphant. The studio clock had relentlessly ticked on and Shannon's time had run out. As she closed the interview, her voice struggled to regain its plumminess. Alison saw from the corner of her eye David's hand leave the arm of his wheelchair and give her a discreet thumbs up. Shannon took off her headphones and smiled icily. Melissa reappeared and hovered.

"Thank you Mr Davidson, Mrs Henderson. I hope you,"

she emphasised the 'you', "got what you wanted from this interview."

"Absolutely. I'm really grateful to you for giving us this opportunity," Alison knew she was gushing, "and I do hope you'll be able to come to our opening, don't you..." she turned questioningly to David but he was gone and her sentence ended with a deflated, "oh". She and Shannon both looked at the space where David had been. Shannon shrugged theatrically and held out her plump hand with its plum-dipped fingers,

"Well goodbye, Mrs Henderson. Melissa will escort you to the lift."

Hurrying back to her car through a fine spring drizzle, Alison was warmed by the glow of the experience she'd just had. What an obnoxious woman! She was clearly motivated only by her own objectives. Thank goodness David had kept the interview focussed on the exhibition and the charity. And how awful it must be if you really are a celebrity and people feel they have the right to pick and choose which parts of you and your life they reveal to the world. She opened the car door with relief and slipped into its dryness. It was all down to David, she thought. He had kept control of the whole thing. Well, what a knight in shining armour! But not even the courtesy of a goodbye. Typical! A little chill seeped into the warmth of her satisfaction.

19

Stress levels rose as the day of the opening drew nearer. Aidan's group of sparrows who could at times be calm, mature, reasonable people were transformed into neurotic obsessives, egocentric tyrants and pathetic wimps.

"I knew it," he complained to Alison. "Always happens. These people have been extracted from the comfort zone of the studio. They feel safe with their mates to whom they revealed their inner creative selves months, if not years, ago. You must know yourself what it's like. Some people are quietly pleased with their efforts and accept praise in a self deprecating way. Some are constantly saying they're hopeless and demanding help. Some work away quietly and diligently and stay at the same level, never seeming to improve but loving what they're doing and some seem to turn up just for the company and something to do. And then you have an exhibition and out come the prima donnas." He lowered his lanky frame onto a plastic chair and stared dolefully at the wall of the Village Hall kitchen.

Alison finished drying mugs at the sink. "We're almost

there now, Aidan. Two days to go. Please don't tell me you're going to do any more rearranging."

"No, I don't think we can. I think it looks really good as it is. I'm hoping all the reasons I've given people are acceptable to them. Virginia said she thought her flower pictures were hidden away in a corner. I think they look charmingly decorative. Roland Wittering-Smythe," his voice took on a lofty tone, "feels his landscapes are hung too close together. I think they work well and give a great identity to his work. Maisie Fullerton has framed hers in such bright colours it was difficult to associate them with anything else but at least they brighten up that area just inside the door and I'm not moving them for anything but Janet Potts has actually crept out of her shell far enough to tell me she thinks I ought to put hers nearer the entrance otherwise she may not sell any. Every single one of them has been to see me privately on behalf of their work. Except you."

"That's probably because I've been too busy. I've been rushed off my feet for days. Hardly had a word to say to Nick and I haven't seen David at all. Have you seen him?" She hung up the tea towel and subsided onto a chair.

"No. Why should I have?"

"I just wondered." She'd ask Nick. Or maybe Maggie.

"He's done everything you asked him to, hasn't he?"

"Oh yes. He has. And some things I didn't ask him to!" She thought of the radio interview. "And I know he'll be here for the gala evening. Kellie-Ann and Nick are helping him."

"Good. So we're all sorted?"

"We are." Irritably, she dismissed David from her mind. "But what a pity about the group. That people aren't satisfied. Is there anything we could do about that?" They looked at each other gloomily.

"I know!" Alison sat up straight. "Why don't we gather in The Huntsman, like we do after the class, and have supper together? We could have that upstairs room. Oh go on, Aidan. Wednesday night. Early doors. Drinks at 6.30 and cottage pie or something simple that Bob does so well. You ring round everyone. You're good at that, making people feel you're their special friend."

"Am I?" Aidan's smile was deeply affectionate as he responded to her enthusiasm. "Is that what you feel, Ali, that I'm your special friend?"

"Of course it is. I mean you are, aren't you? I mean, we are. Friends. You and I are friends."

He reached for her hand, enfolded it with his, drew it to his lips and kissed her palm. "Friends it is, Ali. But I think you know you're much more special to me than just a friend."

Alison withdrew her hand and stood up, collected mugs from the draining board and reached up to put them away in cupboards. "Aidan, I'm so grateful for your friendship. You were there for me when I was miserable and your classes turned my life around; helped me to begin again. You'll never know how much that means to me and I'll always be in your debt."

His chair scraped the floor as he stood up and was beside her, hands on her shoulders, turning her round to face him. He gave her a little shake, then released her. On his face was the look of a man bereft. Alison was alarmed.

"Aidan? Are you all right?" She tentatively put a hand on his arm.

Wearily he leant back against the sink and folded his arms. "No Ali, I'm not all right. But I probably will be because I'm old enough to know that even the broken heart doth mend."

Alison shifted uncomfortably. She knew how painful it would be for her if she had hurt this kind and gentle man.

"Aidan, we have always been honest with one another. You know how it is with me. I was so torn apart when James left me; my feelings were in shreds when I came here. It was hard just to get through the day. It was hard to look at myself in the mirror without seeing myself as a reject. Life was over. But I had to go on for the boys, my grandchildren, the people who love me and with your help some sort of wholeness, a reasonable sense of who I am, has come back to me. But Aidan, dear, dear, Aidan, I honestly haven't got anything to give anyone else. It just isn't here," she held a clenched fist to her chest and bent slightly as if in pain, "and there's still healing to do. This is real life, you know, not a fairytale. There is no magic wand, no happy ever after. There's reality and getting on with stuff. But there's good stuff to get on with, Aidan. And this is good stuff. You and me and our painting friends. We're doing good stuff. So on Thursday, the day before we open, let's have a pre-celebration and go to the pub." She held out her arms and walked towards him. Aidan opened his arms and folded her to him. "Oh there's nothing like a good hug," she mumbled into his sweater. She felt his arms tighten round her briefly, then he kissed the top of her head and let her go.

"OK. You win." His fingers lightly touched her chin and tilted back her head. "Do you know, even with your present through-a-hedge-backwards look you are lovely. And I say this as a friend. You look as though you've been through a hedge backwards."

Alison's laugh was sudden and loud and she felt hugely released by her amusement. "I have been through a hedge backwards, Aidan." She meant it. The pull and tug of emotional ties was a hedge. The ups and downs of a relationship were twigs and thorns she did not want. She did not want to be hedged about with emotional responsibilities and consequences. She wanted Aidan as a friend, but already she felt protective of him and knew she would be careful not to hurt him even if that meant she had to lose his friendship. She smiled broadly at him and took his hand, entwining her fingers with his, fervently hoping she could keep him in her life.

"Come on, good friend. Time for us to shut up shop and for you to start phoning. And don't forget to give Bob a call about the room upstairs."

LATER THAT EVENING, Alison looked critically at her reflection in the mirror. It certainly was a hedge-backwards look. Her hair was unruly, had no shape, and when had the colour become so dull? Tying it back was neat but that was all you could say about it. Her skin, free of makeup, looked healthy but healthy was all very well. How long was it since she'd had a good facial, a decent exfoliate and deep moisturise? She couldn't remember. She scrutinised her face and looked steadily into her own eyes. Honesty, she thought. You've got to be honest. I hope I've been honest with Aidan and not given him any misleading signals. I hope he doesn't feel rejected. She saw the shadow cross her own face as she felt the echo of her pain and knew that though it was subsiding she would have to be careful not to uncover it. She smoothed the skin round her eyes and noticed her shapeless fingernails, felt the roughness of her fingertips. Oh yes. It was certainly time to get well away from that hedge.

20

Warmth and the subtlest fragrance of jasmine enveloped her as the door swished shut and blotted out the noise of traffic splashing through puddles and the grime of the street. She took a deep breath. Lovely. The salon was a vision of glass and pale wood. A simple blind the colour of buttermilk added warmth to the grey morning light. She checked in with the receptionist.

"Please have a seat. Shelley will be right with you."

Alison sank into the irresistible comfort of an oversize chair covered in the palest, softest green fabric. A tall girl with neat and shiny fair hair and a flawless complexion, dazzling white high-necked tunic indicating her professional status, advanced.

"Mrs Henderson?" Her pale pink lips smiled, revealing pearly teeth. "Good morning. It's lovely to have you with us today. I'm Shelley and I'll be taking your details. May I get you something; tea, coffee, juice?"

From the depths of the chair's embrace, Alison smiled. "A cup of coffee would be lovely. Filter, please." This was going to be enjoyable. She would give herself up to the experience of being pampered. It was so long since she'd done this. Where

had she last had a beauty treatment; New York? Hong Kong?
She couldn't recall. But how far away those days of spending
time on her looks were; those days of being representational;
of being someone whose appearance and behaviour was
important. But only important because she was supporting
someone else, she thought. James. She was here today for
herself and that was the biggest luxury of all.

Wrapped in fluffy towelling, all traces of her everyday life
left behind in the cubicle with her jeans and jacket, her shirt
and shoes, Alison gave herself up to the ministrations of the
exquisitely beautiful Shelley and her colleagues. She relaxed on
a warm soft surface and felt skilled fingers caressing and
pummelling with a deep-muscle massage. She drifted to the
sound of the ocean and gentle music which seemed to have no
beginning and no end. Her life, her identity, her responsibilities
were neatly folded in the cubicle with her clothing and she
became part of the ocean, the heavenly music, the scents of
ylang ylang and geranium, frangipani and lavender. Sibilant
words reached her from far away. "Melting tension and stress,"
and "balancing the energy fields of your body."

There was iced mint tea to be sipped and a delicious
smoked chicken sandwich to be nibbled at; then a lime and
ginger salt glow, with body brushing, polishing and softening
and a pro-collagen quartz lift facial. Time slipped past until
eventually she reached the hairdresser's salon and reclined with
her head back over a gleaming white basin, finger- and toenails
immaculate, to begin the last part of her pampering. Water
streamed and foaming lathers and silky conditioners wafted yet
more fragrance and then she was upright, seated in front of a
huge mirror, cuddled by the towelling robe which had become
her home.

"Hola!" Juan Carlos appeared in the mirror, reached for
her hair, running his fingers through it, lifting it, smoothing it,
holding it away from her face, folding it forward. "You have

lovely hair," he smiled, withdrawing his fingers and giving her shoulders a reassuring pat. "So now, what should we do?"

Alison looked at his reflection sleepily and summoned a smile. She felt utterly incapable of making a decision of any kind. "I'm open to suggestion. But whatever we do, it needs to be unfussy. I'm not prepared to spend ages messing about with my hair. It has to be simple and I have to be able to tie it back. Neat. Simple. Healthy. That's it. Oh dear."

"Why 'oh dear'?" A look of concern rearranged Juan Carlos's dark good looks.

"That sounds so boring."

"No, no, no!" His head was gently shaking. "We should do a classic but sharp cut, like this, not too short but defined, and a suggestion of low-lites perhaps, but above all, this is timeless elegance. This is not boring!"

Alison sighed contentedly and smiled at him in the mirror. "That will do nicely," she said.

AT LAST THE big round brush tugged at her hair as Juan Carlos brushed and rolled and pulled, blowing with his dryer which hummed and buzzed as he athletically manoeuvred about the chair, arms now up above her head with the dryer and brush, now down at her jawline; nimble feet carrying him in front of her, behind her, standing back from her to view his work, coming closer to pay attention to detail. Alison could almost hear the guitar and castanets and would not have been surprised by a triumphant *olé*! She watched her hair settle about her face and could see how the expertise of the cut had transformed it and the glow the colour had given her. She smiled radiantly at Juan Carlos.

"Thank you so much. You've done that beautifully."

"*Señora*, the beauty was always there. I am happy you are happy. And instead of the tie-back," he produced a long slender tortoiseshell clip and easily slipped her hair back and up, twisted it slightly and slid in the clip. "Like this. *Si, si!*" He stood back, admiring his own skill.

"I love it," said Alison. Juan Carlos removed the clip and rearranged her hair.

"With my compliments," he said, handing her the clip, "And now, you go to the makeup? Yes?" Alison gathered her robe about her and slipping her feet into her spa slippers, she shuffled in the direction of the makeup. She was getting closer to the cubicle, to her clothes and to her life folded up with them. But this day when her identity had been put aside was a healing day and she felt ready now to shed her temporary anonymity with the towelling robe.

"All our products are natural, using minerals and gentle oils. Now, I think a soft taupe here and maybe some warm coral on the cheeks and to even out the skin tone this lovely tinted moisturiser." Shelley's fingers were deft and she used her brushes and sponges swiftly and skilfully. "You see? Just a touch lighter here under the brows and a little darker here to open the eyes? And really, not too much. You have lovely colouring."

THE TRAFFIC WAS STILL GRINDING its way past but the puddles had dried when Alison stepped out onto the pavement. She felt like skipping. *Where are you, Gene Kelly? I should swing round the lampposts and dance across that pedestrian crossing.* Her attention was grabbed by a large fluorescent sign. Sale. Up to 50% off. *Oh why not! The most up-market boutique in town but how often did she do this?* She walked over the crossing sedately. Closing time was not far off but the assistant smiled bravely as Alison closed the door behind her.

"I'll just have a look, if I may," she said firmly.

"Were you looking for something special, or for a particular occasion?"

"Well it's hard to say what I'm looking for, but I'll know it when I see it." Alison moved hangers along the rails. Why did everything look so limp? And what strange shapes and lengths everything seemed to be. So disappointing.

"Did you want something for everyday wear or perhaps a bit dressy?"

Alison turned to face the assistant. Fatigue was creeping over her. "OK. What do you think would suit me? I'll put myself in your hands."

The woman smiled. "Good idea," she said, sizing Alison up with eyes half-closed. "Right. Come to this fitting room and I'll bring you some things to try. And have courage! Our clothes are unusual, but they're beautifully made and you'll be delighted when you spot what's right for you."

Alison silently obeyed and watched as the assistant returned with shapeless garments of indeterminate colouring draped over her arms. Hangers clicked as she hung them up, festooning the cubicle with charcoal, deep blue, dove grey, berry and brick. Here and there the moodiness was lifted with a hint of chartreuse, a suggestion of iris.

"And the shoes," said the assistant. "Your size?"

THE STREET LIGHTS were illuminated when Alison left the shop, the corded handles of numerous thick paper bags entwined in her fingers. At the crossing the lights were about to change and encumbered as she was, she nevertheless skipped a couple of steps as she headed for her car. Not only had this been a healing day, but she'd been adventuring in the boutique. It's so true, she thought. There are times when retail therapy undoubtedly works.

ALISON PUSHED her way into the upper room at The Huntsman, relieved there was a crush of people. Aidan had clearly used all his charm and gathered everyone. The day had been busy with final preparations for the gala opening the next evening but she'd allowed herself time to get ready for tonight and felt calm and confident that everything was in place. Except David, of course. He was nowhere to be seen and Nick had accused her of fussing.

"Mother, trust me," he'd said with exasperation. "Kellie-Ann and I will have him there at the time you've arranged and we'll stay; we'll hover in the background. You know you can rely on me."

"Yes I do know, darling. But he's such an unknown quantity. He's just a total enigma. What worries me is his unpredictable response to things. I can't tell you how rude he can be, and at all costs I'd like to avoid any confrontation in public."

"There won't be any confrontation. He's just not like that."

"Oh you'd be surprised! With me, he's exactly like that!"

Nick had looked at her sceptically. "But not in public, Mum. I mean, he was an officer after all and he's used to this publicity stuff. He's done it for his books. I think you're making a mountain out of a molehill."

Alison gave him a quick hug. "I'm sure you're right. Thank you for your reassurance. I just would be more confident if I'd had the chance for a mini rehearsal, you know? Showing him where to be and what will happen before the opening and how I want him to do it."

The image of David was before her. His steady grey gaze and his crisp dark hair. She saw the gravity of his face and remembered his wink and smile in the studio. She looked at her son in his faded jeans and disreputable trainers, shirt sleeves rolled up and a button missing.

"Just go with the flow, Mum. Trust him."

She laughed. "Oh I would trust him, Nick, if I had one

shred of evidence that he can be trusted. To be honest, he makes me nervous and I can't adopt your laid-back attitude."

Nick laughed and looked at her shrewdly. "I wonder, Mum, whether it's your own unpredictable response which is making you nervous. Not his."

She stared at him for a moment. "What nonsense. Anyway, I haven't got time for any more of this supposition. Must get on."

"I rest my case." Nick was still smiling at her. "That's so unlike you. You're always so calm and measured and organised. Now you're looking daggers at me."

Instantly contrite, she gave him another hug. "Darling, I'm sorry." She smiled. "You're being such a help to me. I've no right to snap at you. But I do have to get on. Aidan's hopefully gathered everyone at The Huntsman and there's some bonding to be done before tomorrow. I must go and make myself presentable."

"Now it's my turn to say nonsense." Nick's smile was broad. "You look great, Mum. You don't need to be presentable. Just be you."

Alison took a deep breath. "Oh you are so wise for one so young, and, wise man, you speak the truth. That's what I'll be. Or try to."

SHE QUIETLY HOVERED at the edge of the throng, enjoying the buzz of conversation and enjoying having no responsibility this evening. Aidan and his sparrows. What an age it seemed since the first time she'd found herself on the edge of his flock, the outsider looking in, wondering who they were and what it was that gathered them together. Funny, she thought, that now I know who they all are and what gathers them gathers me too, but here I am still on the edge, perching somehow; part of this and yet not part of it. There was Roland with a pint of good ale and Mrs Roland listening to Maisie's habitual earnestness. There was Janet, in command and standing beside Aidan, hand possessively on his arm, attracting his attention. And Virginia, flushed and happy, loving the conviviality.

"Ali!" Virginia's mouth dropped. "Wow! You look so different! What have you done?"

Alison nervously patted the tortoiseshell clip in her hair. "What d'you think? Does it look OK?"

"Turn around. Let me look. It does look very OK. But so different. What happened to the jeans and the fleece and the too busy to bother look?"

Alison laughed. "Did I get that bad? I just pulled myself together and gave myself a treat, that's all."

"Some treat." Virginia shrugged her shoulders in her sensible woolly cardigan. "Let me look at you." She stepped back and took in Alison's asymmetric jacket, its elegant corded button holes and covered buttons. She stretched out a hand to feel the lovely intricate blue fabric and the exquisite stitching across its dropped shoulders. "And the trousers," she said, standing back again with surprise. "What do you call those?"

"These," said Alison, undoing the jacket and sticking out a foot so Virginia could more easily inspect her trousers, "are a hugely new shape and yet harking back to the elegance of Katharine Hepburn with a modern twist because they're shorter. And," she wiggled her foot, "here you see my suede French pumps. I believed every word the stylish sales lady told me." She smiled at Virginia, who threw back her head and laughed.

"But that's not all, is it? The hair colour, the style..."

"Ah. That was Juan Carlos. I put myself into his hands as he instructed me to."

"Did you indeed? Well, it was clearly worth it. You look fantastic."

"Thank you." Alison hugged Virginia impulsively. "I was

given the urge having endured a contest between a neat berry-coloured cardigan and a leopard-print jacket and although the berry cardigan won, I found myself yearning for something less sensible."

"I haven't the slightest idea what you're talking about. Looks as though Aidan wants you."

"Ali, over here." Aidan was beckoning, waving an arm over the heads of the sparrows. He picked up a glass of wine with one hand and pointed theatrically to it with the other.

"Looks as though he's organised a drink for you." Virginia looked closely at Alison.

"How sweet. Don't look at me like that, Virginia. Aidan is my friend, that's all."

"If you say so," murmured Virginia.

ALISON TOOK care to speak with everyone during the evening, giving each an opportunity to raise any issues they might have about the opening but regretfully and firmly denying any possibility of rearranging the pictures. As the simple supper neared its end, Aidan stood, raised his glass and made a short toast to his class, to their joint venture and to the following evening when the show would open.

"So home you go everyone, and we'll meet tomorrow for the big event."

21

Alison slipped her feet into the most expensive shoes she'd ever bought and stood up. They felt fine in spite of the height of the heel. She looked in the mirror. Her black silk jacket, buttoned with a single monumental button at the waist, was bordered at the cuffs and the V-front hem with slender slashes of chartreuse and burgundy. Her slim trousers finished at the ankle. She smiled at her reflection with approval. Simple, hugely stylish and pleasingly unconventional. Thank you Juan Carlos, she breathed as her shiny hair swung into place when she moved her head. She wanted to totally forget her appearance and focus on the task ahead of her. She smiled. But I look OK, she thought. She slipped her narrow gold bangles onto her arm and added a diamond pin to the jacket before carefully negotiating the winding stairs.

The front door flew open and banged shut as Nick arrived. Good-luck cards from Ed and the children, from Sally and from London friends fluttered en masse from the hall table onto the floor. She picked them up fondly.

"Ready Mum? Car's outside." He stared at her. "You look amazing. I haven't seen you so dolled up since...since..." His voice faltered and he cleared his throat. "Well, I remember you looking like that when we were kids...you know." His lopsided smile tugged at her heart as she saw his effort to avoid saddening her with a reference to the past.

"Darling Nick. Thank you. You've given my confidence a wonderful boost." She scooped up her papers and folders from the hall table, "And I'm ready to go."

Pots of bay trees festooned with twinkling lights on either side of the door and a smart banner proclaiming the event transformed the Village Hall. A huge arrow pointed to the field next door indicating car parking and Alison could see the flares around the perimeter of the field. The clattering old swing door was hooked open, revealing an unaccustomed smartness of directional lighting slicing through the interior of the old building. Sleek screens were hung with paintings and the dazzling floor, newly polished and awesomely reflective, gave the comfortable old building a veneer of glamour. Alison smiled at the battered paint on the inside of the hooked back door, defiant in the midst of the borrowed sophistication. She was amused at the kinship she felt with the building. We know what we really are, you and I, she thought, just ordinary and friendly and serviceable. But tonight we have work to do and we'll be doing it for those children who need clean water. She felt like punching the air with her fist and shouting 'yeah', but instead she walked purposely through the door, taking a deep breath of enjoyable anticipation.

"Aidan! How wonderful! Perfect. You look like an artist!"

"I am an artist."

"I know, but look at you! Wonderful velvet jacket, superb floppy bow tie and I do believe you've had your hair done."

Aidan tossed his head theatrically. "Darling, you noticed. I think I look like an ageing rocker but my daughters insisted.

Couldn't keep them away once they knew there was a party and Jess insisted an image must be created. She's in marketing. I think she's launching me like a new brand." Aidan gently took Alison's hand and kissed it. "But who's launching you, may I ask? This is not a country Alison, is it? Where did this look come from? Or was it there all the time and you were hiding it? You look truly stunning."

Alison was moved by the affection and sincerity in his voice and found herself blushing under his steady gaze. Around them the hall was buzzing with young people dressed in black and white, organising trays of canapés, lining up champagne glasses, straightening starched tablecloths.

Alison retrieved her hand. "Let's get to work. Any problems you know about?"

"Nope. The team's in the kitchen and we can call on them as and when. They've done a good job, don't you think?"

"Remarkable. This all looks really professional. I can't believe it's us! It works well, having that gathering area and the champagne bar and I love the ribbon strung between those little bay trees. Shall we walk round together, you and I? This is the lull before the storm. I hope so, anyway. Let's start with your paintings."

They stood in silence looking critically at Aidan's pictures. She saw images of wild flowers in jars on Aidan's kitchen windowsill, bowls of vividly coloured fruit on his scrubbed and empty kitchen table and then in complete contrast a bare oak tree in a winter landscape and then the head and shoulders of an old woman. The brush strokes were determined and power-ful; the colours strong and meaningful and the pictures hovered on the edge of abstraction, sometimes tiptoeing further that way, sometimes appearing solidly conventional.

"They're so good, Aidan. Different. Hugely appealing. I know you won't say so yourself, but they are."

As she turned away from the paintings, a tiny one at the

end caught her eye. It was a delicate pastel portrait. She saw herself, tenderly and finely drawn and recognized the depth of feeling of the artist for his subject. She looked speechlessly at Aidan.

"We'll see," Aidan replied quietly. "In this situation each painting is only as good as the market thinks it is. So come over here and let's review yours. Have you even seen them since they were hung?"

"Well no. I haven't had time. I don't even know which ones you chose in the end." They walked together round the side of the screen and Alison was confronted by her pictures, looking surprisingly large in their simple frames with wide mounts. She relived the experience of painting them as she studied them. There was her garden with the pain of the winter months revealed in dull greys and purples, moody shadows and monochrome tonal depths. Paint sagged sadly down her garden door at dusk and dripped despondently from the eves of her clock tower in the rain. There were shadows of late afternoon cast by her shabby old garden gloves, a broken clay pot on the path and discarded newspaper blown against the weeds by the shed and wrapped about a rotting fence-post. She was surprised at the contrast of the brightening of the spring light and colour creeping in; shadows softer, aspects more open. Muddy brown earth was enlivened with energetic bright green bulb spears piercing upwards against a pale sky and next to it a picture of the old wall with creeper coming to life; a tender green unfurling against the apricots and russets of the bricks. Extraordinary she'd never noticed how her painting reflected the lifting of her mood; the easing of her pain. "And the plucky little tree," she laughed. "I really love that tree. It was Jake's inspiration. But I never thought of it as plucky. I thought of it as a shelter for the birds and saw it as a haven for me, I suppose. I'll be sitting under it when it's fully grown and I'm old and doddery and the birds will still be there. D'you know," she turned from the picture and smiled at Aidan with delight, "that tree has something of interest about it at every season. In the winter its shape is a delight and the shininess of its bark reflects any twinkle of sun that's going. It looks entrancing with frost on it." She turned back to the picture; traced its shape in the air with an imaginary brush. "Then there's really pretty white blossom in the spring and lovely leaves which start off a pinky colour and go glossy green in the summer and then in autumn they're like small flames. Superb. It seems to attract people, that tree." They stood in silence. "Even David paused under it," she said at last. She felt a prickle of anxiety. She wished he'd make his appearance. "I'm gushing, aren't I?" She glanced up at Aidan. "Come on. We really don't have time to luxuriate in our own brilliance. To work!"

THE NOISE LEVEL increased as cars drew up, doors slammed, voices were raised in greeting. The young staff hovered expectantly, trays at the ready. Alison watched from behind the bay trees as local people and strangers she'd never seen before made their way into the hall. She saw the mad scurry of the bar staff checking their bottles in big tubs of ice, bringing trays of canapés from the kitchen, straightening a crooked glass, stitching a smile onto an anxious face. The raffle table was stunning, with a huge showy ribbon-tied bunch of flowers in shiny cellophane, some glossy green plants waving gently as people passed, serious bottles of wine, a totally over-the-top basket of fruit, some beribboned hampers and a collection of intriguing and very flash envelopes containing star prizes. Aidan stood quietly, hands loosely clasped together, unusually glossy hair framing his calm face. Alison gave him a small wave and he smiled and winked. They were ready. The artists had all arrived and were fortified with a glass of champagne. Maisie was flushed and Roland already talking too loudly.

"This all looks wonderful Ali," said Virginia.

Her classic little black dress and family pearls were so predictable, thought Alison, but so Virginia and so endearing. She gave her friend a squeeze. "Virginia, all I need to know right now is that your brother-in-law is going to do what's expected of him."

"Oh he will," and Virginia rushed away to meet and greet. Alison kept her eye on the door. There was Shannon Greenburg, tiers of the finest midnight jersey expensively skimming and slimming her bulk, the effect made even more successful with a shiny contrasting shawl draped over one shoulder. Alison remained where she was as Shannon oozed up to Aidan for an official greeting. The hall was nearly full. The press were apparent and who was Aidan greeting? Alison watched speculatively. Might they be from galleries? Maybe from London? Who knew. She needed David to be here. Where was Nick with David?

ALISON FACED the expectant crowd of people and could see their expectation become tinged with irritation as the first glasses were emptied and still nothing had happened. People were getting restive. Her heart began to race as she realized she would have to take action. Swiftly she went through her options. Should she stall and apologise, say there was a short delay, or should she just go ahead and start the proceedings herself? She tried to calm her intense annoyance that David had failed to meet this obligation; tried to be calm as she formulated the short speech she would make. A quiet began to fall as people stopped talking and turned towards her and the hush became expectant. She met the gaze of the crowd in front of her, quickly cleared her throat and took a deep breath. All at once the talking stopped and silence fell. Alison felt a movement beside her. She turned just as David completed his final steps to her side. He stood tall and straight, his powerful frame restrained by a black dinner jacket; his immaculate white shirt finished with discreet crested studs. David looked down at Alison and smiled. He bent towards her confidentially.

"Good evening, Madam," he whispered. "This narrow squeak of an arrival wasn't intentional. Nick and I underestimated the walk from over there to here." Alison was speechless. In the shadows behind David, she could see Nick folding the wheelchair. David moved his walking frame to one side, keeping a hand resting on it, and turned to face the audience with a dazzling smile. There was a spontaneous burst of applause. David wordlessly inclined his head in acknowledgement and turned again to Alison. She was irritated beyond belief at his late arrival. Her confidence was shaken by his pre-emption of her introduction and it seemed to her that his conceit with the achievement of his walk was complete as he gazed down at her. But he had done it, she thought. He had demonstrated his vulnerability in public, had taken a risk. She found her composure in tatters and her plan erased from her mind. Silence lengthened. Wordlessly she turned and faced the audience. It was the look on Shannon Greenburg's face, a look which clearly said 'this is what happens when mere amateurs try to get something done', which galvanised her. She smiled and took a deep breath, grateful that Aidan had swiftly come to join her.

"Ladies and gentlemen," she began clearly, her voice tinged with the silvery steel of her irritation, "I know you will be as delighted as I am that David Rowbottom...that is, Hal Davidson, has been able to join us this evening. On behalf of Cleanwater I give you heartfelt thanks for being here and for supporting this excellent cause and we all, Aidan Forester our tutor and all the members of the Highvale Art Group, hope you will enjoy our efforts which we've brought together for this exhibition. Now I'm sure you've waited quite long enough," she turned to David with a smile, "So please will you welcome again Hal Davidson." She took a small step away from David and gave him the floor. Her heart was racing and the palms of her hands were damp as she gratefully felt Aidan's lean frame beside her. She knew it! She just knew David would do something like this. Well, the sooner he did what he'd been asked to do the better. It was time to get the evening going.

DAVID WAITED CALMLY for the applause to cease and then spoke.

"Your reception has been most kind and entirely undeserved," he said. "The people who deserve your applause are Alison Henderson and Aidan Forester who have put together this exhibition for this enormously worthwhile cause. You may or may not be aware that I have a deeply felt reluctance to make personal appearances in public but when I was asked to do this, by Mrs Henderson's committee, I thought I'd have a look at this charity before I decided to support it. This I have done and I'm astonished at how much can be effectively achieved if funds are available, in terms of saving children's lives, preventing the spread of disease, bringing rural communities together, fostering people's own self-reliance and restoring their self-respect. Loss of self-respect is something I know a lot about. I know how it breeds hopelessness and turns your life into a monochrome dead end. All joy, all brightness, all colour is absent." He paused and said quietly, "This I know. This has been my experience too. But sometimes colour can be brought back into your life," he made a wide gesture with his arm, embracing the pictures surrounding him, "and this evening you see before you a gift from the Highvale Art Group, the gift of colour. Here are pictures which will delight you and brighten your lives. And here beside me is a person who has brightened and brought colour back into my life." He turned and stretched out his hand towards Alison. She stood still and looked at it, confused. "Please take my hand," he whispered. Wordlessly Alison moved towards him and put her hand in his, felt his gentle, powerful grasp; felt the intention of his action. David drew her towards him. Holding her hand firmly in his he said to her, "Thank you, Madam, for the colour you have brought into my life." Did her heart stop briefly when he winked almost imperceptibly? How gentle his smile was. What was that he'd said? How blue his eyes looked. Would her feet ever move again? There was silence, "And now, may I say that the exhibition is open?" he asked, his eyes not leaving her face. She nodded, unmoving.

"Someone needs to move the bloody bay trees," she said to David as he formally declared the exhibition open and instantly regretted her words as he clearly wouldn't be that someone. But Nick was there moving the trees aside and people began to flow past them. Aidan took her elbow and guided her to one side and she saw Nick hover as David made his way to a chair. What had he said? Why had he said it? Why had he been so personal? Why wasn't she furious? She looked at Aidan as though for answers but he was watching David with a fascinated stare like a rabbit caught in headlights.

"Come on, Ali." His tone was strangled, "We'll have to mingle. Is the selling team organised? I'll keep tabs on the guys from the galleries. You do the rest."

ALISON'S ATTENTION returned to the job in hand. She smiled and mingled and listened. She sipped champagne and tried a canapé and mingled some more. She applauded the raffle winners and congratulated an ecstatic Maisie on her first sale. Small red dots began to appear on the pictures as they were sold. At last the hall began to empty.

"Let me know when you're ready to leave, Mum." Nick was

beside her, car keys jangling in his hand. Alison put down her glass and kicked off her shoes. It was over. The battered old door banged shut. She looked round the empty hall. Lights were being switched off and doors locked. She picked up her shoes.

"I'll just get my things." She smiled gratefully at Nick.

"Celebration glass in The Huntsman?" Aidan looked as tired as she felt. She shook her head. "Until morning then. Here? Eleven o'clockish?"

She nodded. She could see Nick outside, van door open, engine revving. Again she nodded.

"I never thanked David," she said as she headed gratefully for Nick's van and home.

22

Alison was instantly energised when she woke. The exhibition had been a success. She couldn't wait to see how much they had made. Feet feeling for her slippers and impatient to get on with the day, the image of David was suddenly in her head and her heart raced. Damn. She found the slippers and forced her thoughts to regroup. Brushing her teeth she heard his words, 'you brought colour back into my life'. She rinsed her mouth and spat forcefully. So charming. Glib, really. Clearly totally at ease in front of an admiring crowd. What nonsense to say he didn't like public appearances. She brushed her hair and twisted it to accept Juan Carlos's elegant clip, looking at herself critically. David had hijacked her introduction. Her eyebrows rose indignantly. She stuck the clip into her hair and secured it. Her critical expression changed to outrage. How conceited and overbearing can one person be? Why could he not just have appeared, allowed her to introduce him and make her small speech and then open the bloody exhibition? Infuriating. Her excitement turned to irritation before she had her first sip of coffee. But at least it's over, she thought, taking milk out of the fridge and slamming the door. I don't have to work with him again, speak with him again, even see him again. She poured the milk slowly into her coffee and sighed deeply.

She remembered how he'd suddenly been there beside her and, in spite of the dinner jacket and the glamour, instantly she recalled the grounded flyer he'd been at The Stables and the insistent protector he'd been at the radio studio. She could feel the firm clasp of his hand and how she'd stood, dumb, and let him make his ridiculous statement. Dumb, she thought, fighting the feeling of warmth and softness which was creeping over her. I'm dumb, stupid. I stood there in front of all those people, said not one word, and let him carry on. Well, that's enough. I don't have to see him again, of course. But then again I might; in the village. Stirring the coffee, she smiled a tiny smile which broadened as she remembered she had yet to thank David. I do still have that to do. After all, he did lend us his name and his fame, and it's only polite to offer thanks for that.

AIDAN WAS WAITING for her when she arrived at the Village Hall, arms open and smiling broadly.

"Come here my beloved best friend," he said and enveloped her with a hug, burying her face in his comfortable old jumper.

She laughed as she came up for air. "My goodness. Such affection so early. What is this in aid of?" Silently Aidan took her hand and led her to where his paintings hung. He stood, arms folded, looking at the pictures. Alison looked at him, then at the pictures then back at him. She waited.

"Don't you see? Look! Look at the pictures!"

"I am looking at them. Why do you want me to look at them?"

He grunted with exasperation. "What do they all have

stuck on them that wasn't there this time yesterday?" Aidan was pointing. Alison squeaked.

"Aidan. You've sold them all. Each one has a red dot. That's fantastic. Congratulations."

He grabbed her hand again and marched round the corner of the screen. "And look at these." She looked at her own paintings. Each one had gained a small red dot.

"Oh Aidan," she said quietly, awe in her voice, "I can't believe that. People actually paid for my paintings?"

"Not only paid, Ali, but paid full whack and," he was pulling something out of his wallet and handing it to her, "this is who will be getting in touch with you." She looked at the small white card engraved in black with 'Turvil and Neale. Fine Art'.

She looked uncomprehendingly at him and asked, "Do they want us to stage an exhibition for them?"

Aidan laughed. "I think we'd better sit down. Let's go and have another fabulous Village Hall coffee and I'll fill you in."

THE REALITY of the plastic chair she was sitting on, the feel of the thick serviceable mug she was drinking from, the sound of the dripping tap and the sudden sporadic whir of the extractor fan receded as Aidan talked.

"Felix Turvil could see instantly the reaction your paintings were having and how fast they were selling. He bought some himself but is really interested in taking you on and encouraging your painting. Alison, you made thousands of pounds last night. I know some will go to Cleanwater, of course, but it's the potential I'm talking about. Didn't I say you really have something?"

Alison put down her mug and felt the firmness of the table with her hands and shifted her feet to feel the steadiness of the floor as she tried to grasp reality. "I'm not sure I understand the significance of this, Aidan. It's not as though I'm some young thing panting for a career or starving in a garret for the sake of my art. This is my hobby, a pastime, not a career. I'll obviously wait until this man contacts me, if he does. But it's very nice to know this has happened and even nicer to know we made some money for Cleanwater."

Aidan looked deflated. "Ali, this is the most exciting thing that's happened to me in a long time. I'm excited for you! Here you are, valiantly pulling yourself out of the awful hole that bugger of a husband chucked you into and here's this amazing opportunity in front of you. It's fantastic! It's a reward for all your hard work! It's a discovery of your talent, your ability. For me, this is nothing short of amazing."

As Aidan spoke, Alison was remembering David's words; 'all joy is absent', 'monochrome dead end'. She recalled the pinched look on his face when he'd described loss of self-respect and hopelessness, how he'd gritted his teeth and the tiny twitch at the corner of his mouth. What if he really meant what he said? She saw his smile when he said 'you brought colour into my life', and remembered how his smile had reached his grey eyes and kept her speechless.

"Aidan, I don't think I can listen to any more right now. I'm feeling confused. Let's just get on with what we have to do, shall we, and wait and see what happens. I would like to keep my feet very firmly on the ground. Recovering from life's knocks is a struggle and I have no wish to be back in what you call that hole again. Dashed hopes and shattered dreams are painful. It's better to have neither."

As she pushed back her chair and stood up, Alison rather violently shoved David Rowbottom out of her mind.

23

E vents moved far more swiftly than she could have imagined. The local TV news tracked her down and interviewed her about the exhibition and her personal success. Felix Turvil phoned to say he was in the area and could he visit her at The Stables and she agreed, thankful that Nick was at home when he came.

"I know nothing about this world, Nick. I feel adrift, somehow, and I'm not going to agree to anything. I'll just listen."

ALISON LIKED Felix Turvil at once. He was slight and sandy-haired, his jeans immaculate, shoes shiny and well-cut jacket a clever trendy take on classic tweed. His self-confidence was tangible and his friendly 'Hi there. I'm Felix,' amused and attracted her. There was clearly only one Felix in his world. He was not a lot older than Nick, but, initial greetings completed, as he got down to business, she could see a sharp and intelligent mind as well as expertise and authority in his business world. She began to see he was as passionate about his world of art as Nick was about his cars. Nick was silent, listening, looking slightly bemused.

"So, Mrs Henderson..."

Alison shook her head. "Alison will be fine, Felix."

He smiled and acknowledged her request. "Alison. Thank you. So what do you feel about taking your painting seriously and spending some time doing it and planning a way forward?"

"Felix, I'm going to be totally honest with you. This is not something I expected to be doing. I'm the age I am and I've reached a certain place in my life." She glanced at Nick who was hanging on to every word. "I'm delighted our Cleanwater project has been such a success but really, painting is a hobby for me and I'm not looking for another big project or a career or anything like that. To be honest, I'm not even looking for what you might call a new income stream. If I was to take painting seriously maybe I'd think of taking some sort of course, be a mature student or something. Aidan has been fantastic of course, but I do feel I'm something of a novice."

She was aware of Felix listening attentively as she rolled ideas around and voiced them. Then she gave herself a mental shake. "What nonsense! Felix, this is just a hobby for me. I'm hugely flattered by your attention and your encouragement but I think that's probably all it will be."

"Mum," Nick stood up and ran his fingers through his disordered hair. "I think you need to hear more of what Felix has to say. Don't write yourself off too soon."

"I don't think I'm writing myself off, Nick." She was indignant. "I'm making a life choice. There's nothing wrong with opting for the enjoyment of an absorbing hobby."

"Mum, please just listen. I can see Felix has a lot more to say. I'll heat the coffee up." He picked up the pot and headed for the kitchen. "But I can hear you, Felix. Carry on."

Alison relaxed back into her chair. "OK, Felix. I'll listen.

But my son Ed and his family will be here in a couple of hours, so forgive me if I tell you my time is limited."

Felix smiled, crossed one leg neatly over the other, brightening the room with a flash of coloured stripy sock and kept his mild and intelligent gaze completely focussed on Alison. He outlined a sponsorship deal which would benefit not only Turvil and Neale but also Alison and Cleanwater. There was silence as Nick poured more coffee and passed mugs around.

"You want me to go to Africa?" Alison heard her voice squeak with disbelief. "Why on earth would you pay all that money and trust a complete amateur like me? I've never painted in Africa! You have no idea what the outcome would be and what if no one wanted to buy them? It sounds ridiculous to me."

"Alison, Turvil and Neale was started by my grandfather. My Dad is still very much involved and as you can see, it's my passion too. We have been very fortunate. As a family we're fortunate. I'm not saying that everything we do is for the good of mankind. No. We need to make money too. But my Dad has been involved with Africa for years and we have close links with Cleanwater. I'd be using your gift to fundraise for Cleanwater. We'd give you all the support you need, travel, equipment, tuition, whatever you ask for, and you would paint, just as you have done here, and your painting would be used for cards and posters and bookmarks and whatever else the merchandisers dream up. The point is, your gift is not just the technical skill you have. You are also part of a story, and the story has a value in itself. You are able to get emotion into your painting which is quite unique and would lend itself perfectly to this purpose. I'm being totally honest. This is a commercial proposition. We will benefit from tax issues and publicity. Cleanwater will benefit from the same plus from fundraising and you will be exploring your talent and seeing the world."

"I've already seen a lot of the world," Alison looked at him speculatively, "possibly a bit too much. I'm really settled here, where I am."

Felix looked at Nick, who shrugged his shoulders.

"Is that a no, Mum? Are you not even going to consider it?"

Felix got out his laptop and Nick made a space on the table. "Have a look, Mum. Don't say anything yet. And anyway, you may want to talk to Ed when he comes this afternoon."

Alison glanced round the big comfy room and a satisfying glimpse of her garden caught momentarily in slanting sunshine was framed in the arched windows. She sat down and prepared to give Felix her attention. On his screen she watched the scenes of smiling villagers, school children, flat landscapes with big skies, round dwellings with thatched roofs. She remembered the feel of Africa; the vastness of the landscapes, coolness of early mornings in safe suburbs with well tended gardens, overwhelming crowdedness and piles of rubbish, corrugated iron and plastic dwellings in city slums. Felix talked her through the projects his slideshow illustrated and Turvil and Neale's contribution to the merchandise. He stopped talking and paused his slideshow.

"What d'you think so far?"

Alison hesitated before replying. "I absolutely applaud what you and your company do and you know I have huge admiration for Cleanwater, but to be honest I can't see that your proposal is for me. The problem is, Felix, I'm content to be where I am and doing what I'm doing." She looked at Nick and said, "I've been through an enormous upheaval in my life and I'm just beginning to feel settled. I don't know that I want to uproot myself, either physically and go off to Africa, or in my lifestyle and get involved in the pressures of deadlines or becoming a student. I'm a granny, Felix, and when you're my age priorities alter. There's a huge amount of joy to be found in many small things in life without having to have massive ambition or challenging personal goals."

She smiled calmly at the two earnest young men who immediately engaged each other with despairing looks which quickly became speculative as they re-grouped to find another means of persuasion. Alison watched Felix's fingers fly over his keyboard, Nick looking over his shoulder, nodding.

"Wow," said Nick, "where is that?"

"Lovely, isn't it?" Felix turned the computer slightly, improving Alison's view and drawing her in. "This is where you'd stay before flying to our various projects in the region." Alison saw a big rambling thatched building with sturdy walls, some rough hewn and some painted bright white. There were wide lawns, rows of agapanthus and views over the bush. She saw a simple bedroom with crisp white sheets and a shiny copper bath, rooms with thick tree trunks emerging through wide wooden floorboards and supporting arching rafters. "Some of our projects are within a day's flying. Here's the plane and the airstrip." She saw the little airstrip, windsock fluttering, and bright yellow light aircraft. "We'd give you all the support you'd need, some initial tuition if you like, bag carriers for your equipment; take someone with you! A companion? And please don't worry about deadlines. There are deadlines, of course, because we have to make commitments, but again, there are so many ways we can help there too."

Alison laughed and pushed back her chair. Felix and Nick exchanged bewildered looks.

"Felix, it all looks absolutely lovely and what a thrilling adventure you're offering me. I still totally fail to take it all in and grasp why you're doing this but I can see what a marvellous opportunity it is. It's all so unexpected and I suppose I just have to have a little time to think about it, think whether I can see myself in this role, if you like, and see myself making the commitment you require."

"Mum!" Nick exploded. "What do you mean 'see yourself in this role'? What role are you talking about?"

"Well, the role of professional painter, I suppose. Professional painter and traveller."

"And what have you been for the last God knows how many years; for the whole of your married life? Professional traveller for goodness' sake!" He shoved a hand through his hair, speechless with exasperation. Alison felt her heart squeezed by the objectivity of his reference to her married life but warmed by his interest in and concern for her. She felt a calm settle over her. This was her decision and she needed time. She smiled at the two young men.

"You are both complete darlings to be so concerned for me and I really appreciate it. But I do need time. Let me think about it. I still have commitments and loose ends to tie up after our exhibition, and Ed and Giselle will be here soon. Felix, please stay for supper. It'll be early because of the children. You'd have plenty of time to get back to London."

Felix closed his laptop gently. "Thank you Alison, but I have to get back and I'm sure it would be better if you talked to your family without me." He slipped his computer into his bag and held out his hand. "Thank you for listening to me and you can rely on me keeping my fingers crossed that I'll be hearing from you in the next couple of days. If I don't, may I call you?"

"Of course. But I won't keep you waiting."

"This is what it's all about." Alison raised her glass and looked round her table at her family. "It's all about you guys and I love it and here's to all of you. It's so nice to have you all here together." The children laughed and clinked glasses. "I'm sorry Kellie-Ann couldn't join us, Nick."

"Well, Mum, I think we should be raising a glass to you,"

Ed smiled at her, "to congratulate you. We are all really delighted about your success and so proud of you."

"Absolutely!" Giselle joined in. "This offer from Turvil and Neale sounds fabulous."

Alison got up and began clearing plates, helped by Chloe. "We'll see. I'm thinking about it. Thank you Chloe. Let's go and get the pudding, shall we?" No. No, no, she thought. No enthusiastic encouragement thank you Giselle. Let me just enjoy being with you all. But when she and Chloe got back to the table she could see there was to be no escape.

"It's like a dream come true, isn't it Alison? You remember that talk we had, about being your own person and doing what fulfils you, yourself?"

"Oh yes, I do remember," she said, spooning meringue and cream and soft fruit into bowls. "And very helpful it was, Giselle, at the time." She looked meaningfully at her daughter-in-law.

Giselle smiled winningly. "Nick tells us you're giving Felix Turvil's offer some thought."

"Yes." Alison was brief, hoping to end the conversation.

"But what is there to think about? This is exactly what you needed; a purpose in life, something for you to excel at, to enjoy, to be absorbed by."

Alison could feel irritation begin to prickle. "I have already explained to Felix and Nick," she looked meaningfully at Nick, "that I enjoy what I'm doing right now. I love it here in High-vale and I love being a granny," she smiled and winked at the children, "and I love my hobby and my local friends. I think I'm very fortunate and I'm beginning to feel rooted," she ended triumphantly. "So none of you need to worry about me. I'm fine."

"But that's just how you're feeling now," persisted Giselle. "And you're stereotyping yourself, this 'granny living in the country doing domestic things' role. That's not the real you."

The irritation was beginning to firm up into something more solid. "Do we ever know who we really are, Giselle? Don't you think we change according to age and circumstance? I think we also should be careful we don't get confused between what really is the real us and what is in fact other people's image of what they think is the real us."

There was silence. Ed and Giselle and Nick, wide-eyed and suddenly tense, focussed on Alison. The children asked if they could leave the table. Alison burst out laughing.

"What did I say? Did anyone understand a word I said? All this stuff is confusing me totally. All I need is time. Tomorrow I'll tie up all the loose ends from the exhibition and I promise I'll give it lots of thought."

24

It was a spur-of-the-moment decision. Alison walked through the village to collect her milk and newspaper. She walked briskly, enjoying the familiarity of her surroundings and returning cheerful waves as cars passed. She reached the turning to The Glebe. On impulse she turned left off the main road into The Glebe and towards David's house. Might as well do it personally, she thought. Get the thank you over with and it's done. No need to write a formal letter.

She was annoyed at the sudden racing of her heart as she walked towards the front door. No sign of the Trailblazer. Impatiently, she rang the doorbell and heard it echo through the house. It was an empty sound. She pressed the bell again. No response. She paused as her mood plummeted and then, giving herself a sensible mental shake, she turned and headed back to the road. A letter of thanks it would have to be. Then she stopped in disbelief. Planted in the middle of the small lawn in front of David's house was a 'To Let' sign. She stared at it. Surely not. It must be the neighbour's. She glanced at the hedge between the houses. No. It was on this side of the hedge, on David's lawn. This is ridiculous, she thought. Why should he want to let his house? Suddenly aware of how long she'd been standing in the drive looking at the sign, she glanced briefly back at the house and then walked down the drive and headed for The Stables, newspaper and milk forgotten.

"Virginia! Thank goodness you're in." She heard her breathlessness as Virginia answered the phone.

"Alison. Lovely to hear from you. Are you OK? You sound a bit breathless."

"I'm fine, thanks. I'm just finishing everything off after the exhibition, and one of the things I have to do is thank David."

"That's really sweet of you, especially knowing your feelings about him."

"My feelings? What do you mean, my feelings?"

"Well the fact you don't like him, of course. You certainly made it clear to me that the two of you don't get on at all."

"Ah, that. Yes. But we do appreciate the help he gave us with the exhibition."

"I thought he did the opening with great charm, didn't you Alison? Brief, maybe, but he's never liked the limelight, and he seemed to get everything off to a good start."

"Well yes, of course, and I'm grateful which is why I wanted to say thank you. But I went to see him this morning and it appears his house is for rent."

She held her breath, waiting for Virginia's answer.

"That's right. He's gone on a book tour. He left the morning after the exhibition."

"A tour? How long is a tour? And why did he have to let his house?"

"Alison, darling! Why all this interest? I thought you couldn't care less about David. You could always write the letter and leave it with me and I'll forward it. Or you could email."

There was silence. Alison pulled herself together.

"Thank you, Virginia. I'll do one or the other. 'Bye now." She put down the phone, suddenly feeling overwhelmingly tired and drained of energy. The phone rang, making her jump. It was Giselle, thanking for supper and uttering soothing and dutiful noises about Alison's decisions being respected by them all and that she must take care of herself and give herself some 'me time' after all her hard work.

Feeling at least one hundred by the time Giselle had finished, Alison gently replaced the phone, drooped her way to the kitchen and collapsed onto a chair. 'Me time', she thought. Whatever is 'me time'? David had left, without even a goodbye. Oh you fool, you fool, Alison. She ran a distracted hand through her hair. The echo of James' rejection was creeping up on her. But David hadn't rejected her! What was she thinking? Oh this was without doubt a narrow escape. She had almost felt sorry for him when he'd so openly expressed his thanks to her. How easily one can be charmed by that 'lame duck' thing. And I certainly did feel sympathy, she thought, as she recalled his valiant struggle to stand and walk; his open revelation about his ejection from his aircraft and his obvious distress over the death of his fellow pilot. Of course she'd felt sympathy. Well, if he had gone on a book tour he was clearly no lame duck. She watched the rain bouncing off the flagstones in the garden. She felt the need for action. Damn it, she was going to take Felix's offer. And right now!

FELIX TURVIL WAS true to his word and before long she was packed and booked and ready to go. Then she told her family. They were surprised and anxious that she hadn't consulted them, kept them informed, asked their opinions. But Nick was happy to take care of The Stables, no doubt with the help of Kellie-Ann. Aidan was not so happy, as she'd expected.

"You are sure you're not being hasty, Ali? This isn't a knee-jerk reaction?"

"Reaction to what? It's a lovely offer and Felix has been very thorough and I feel very well looked after. You encouraged me, Aidan! You yourself said it was a lovely offer."

"I know. But I'll miss you, my beloved friend." He came close to her and tenderly stroked her cheek, looking closely at her face, absorbing her image with an artist's intensity. She could see his pain, feel his sense of loss.

"I'm coming back, Aidan," she whispered. "Please don't be sad."

"It won't be the same." His smile was tight and his voice cracked a little. "My bird with the broken wing will fly and who knows what she'll see from new and dizzy heights." He held her face in both his hands and bent to kiss her, a butterfly brush on her lips and then a gentle lingering resting of his mouth on hers as he absorbed the essence of her, breathed her in. In a moment it was over and she was enveloped in one of his bear hugs, her cheek against the ancient wool of his jumper, her ear hearing the way his heart raced. As he released her she felt unsteady and instantly his hand was on her arm, steadying; his face was absorbed concern. She saw the depth of his feeling for her and as though light dawned, she realised how rare and precious it was.

"Darling Aidan," he winced at the endearment, "but you are a darling! You have done so much for me, helped me to find something from deep down that I didn't know I had. And it would be such a pity not to go on, wouldn't it? You of all people will surely support me?"

"Ali, I have never told you anything but the truth. You don't need my support. You don't need anyone's support. Now's the time for you to go and do this for yourself..."

He was silent as Alison held up her hand to halt him. "Please don't tell me this is my 'me time'," she laughed. "It is simply a lovely opportunity and in spite of small anxieties and a little nervousness, I'm going. To the sun! To Africa! And Aidan," she put her hand in her pocket and pulled out a smart-phone, "I have global roaming and I'll be keeping in touch."

He smiled and nodded. "Good. That'll be good," he said softly.

25

Highvale seemed very far away very quickly. I'm like a snail, thought Alison, winkled out of my shell. My lovely Stables are way up there in the north, and here am I heading south. Adventuring. She'd placed herself and her immediate future in the hands of others: Felix who had organised the whole trip and now the pilots on the flight deck of this aircraft. Pilots. Aviators. Men who flew. David. But you don't fly anymore, do you David. Well, we all have times in our lives when we can't do what we want to do; can't have what we want. And if we all went around carrying chips on our shoulders as large as yours, David Rowbottom, what a sad place the world would be. She stretched out her legs and wiggled her feet and resolutely looked forwards, closing her mind to the past. Next stop Johannesburg and then the bush.

THE FOLLOWING DAY, strapped into her seat in a much smaller aircraft bereft of stretching or toe-wiggling room, the African panorama absorbed Alison and she found herself considering greens and greys, shadows and light, scars of red earth left behind by powering floodwater, distant blue mountains and the cerulean arc of the sky. The aircraft banked and steadied and she saw the airstrip below, small hangers and a windsock, a minute control tower and the sun glinting off windscreens of parked vehicles. She smelt Africa as soon as the door was opened; dustiness, dryness, hot tarmac and aviation fuel. She held onto the rail of the steps with one hand and in the other clutched her bag, gripping her jacket and pashmina awkwardly under her arm.

"Mrs Henderson," with a wide smile and a helping hand a member of the staff from Golongwe greeted her, took her bag and her winter woollens, escorted her to a liveried Land Rover. Warm wind blew through her hair on the drive to Golongwe and caressed her bare arm resting on the door and she felt the dust from the road settle between her fingers.

THE LAND ROVER stopped in front of the Lodge, so much part of its landscape that Alison was surprised they'd arrived. The dust cloud settled as the door was opened for her.

She was deposited in a room built of Africa, rough-hewn stone, weathered tree trunks supporting the walls and arching up to the roof and a floor of smoothly planed planks. There was crisp white bed linen and a soft grey rug, a large sofa adorned with cushions, a fireplace with logs in it and the shiniest most luxurious bathroom possible. The huge window revealed a breathtaking view across well-cut lawns to the bush and the distant escarpment. Pushing aside the enormous sliding pane of glass, Alison walked out onto her private veranda and drew a deep breath. It was late afternoon. A tray of tea waited serenely on a small table and she sank into a chair and poured steaming liquid into a thin white china cup. This was lovely. She sipped the tea appreciatively and let her surroundings wash over her. She kicked off her shoes. She was wearing too many clothes. She couldn't wait to get in the shower and let warm water wash away the dust of travel, the smell of aircraft, the tension of moving from one place to another.

RESPITE FROM TENSION was brief and next morning Alison felt her nervousness build as she sorted out her painting kit and checked her camera. She was to be met at breakfast by her guide before heading off into the wilderness which stretched in all directions from Golongwe.

On the shaded veranda at the front of the lodge she paused, conscious of her unfamiliar lightweight clothing, her bare arms, her travelling clutter in bags slung over both shoulders, her hat clutched anxiously in one hand. From the depths of the shade came a slight figure, hand outstretched in greeting.

"Alison? Hello. I'm Fantasia." The voice was deep and rich. The figure was tiny. Alison took the hand of the small wrinkled person in front of her. Everything was wrinkled. Her face, her arms, her big linen shirt, her sand coloured trousers. Even her wiry grey hair was wrinkled in spite of being dragged into a knot on top of her head.

"Hello," said Alison.

Fantasia laughed, a laugh which shook her whole being.

"Don't look so puzzled. I'm your artistic support. Felix arranged for me to come along with you. Come and have some breakfast. Your guide and driver are waiting outside for us." She shepherded Alison to a table, stowed the equipment and indicated the buffet. The small wiry Fantasia, in spite of her apparent advanced years, moved with spritely energy and pulled up a chair and poured the coffee.

"Go on. Get some fruit, some juice. Try the yoghurt, made here, and the waffles. This place is famous for the waffles."

Alison obeyed, so intrigued by Fantasia that painting anxiety evaporated.

"Good." Fantasia's bird-like hands fluttered in applause as Alison sat down with creamy yoghurt, fresh orange juice, papaya, waffles. "We have no idea when we'll eat again, so it's just as well to make the most of breakfast. And now, your face is still puzzled. Who am I, is that what you're thinking?"

Alison straightened up, embarrassed. "Well no, that is..."

Fantasia's head was on one side, one eyebrow raised, smiling broadly. Alison relaxed. "Well yes," she confessed, "Felix said he'd organise someone to give me advice but..."

"But you hadn't expected an ancient old body like me," Fantasia finished for her. She held up her hand as Alison began to protest and then leaned forward conspiratorially. "It's all a ruse. I'm pretty old, of course, but not as old as I look. I've lived all my life in this African sun and now I get so much more help and so much kindness because of my age. They really respect age in this country." Her eyes twinkled. "So here I am, an old Africa hand and just delighted to be part of this Clean-water project. And I know you're going to have a lovely time and achieve great results." She reached across the table and patted Alison's hand. "So, in your kit have you plenty of reds, oranges, yellows, purples, blues as well as browns and greens? I presume you're going to use pans of watercolour. So much more immediate than oils or acrylics and much easier to use when time is of the essence."

"I'm going to take photos too," Alison said somewhat weakly in the face of all this energy. "I'm not experienced in either photography or painting from photos but Felix seemed to think this was a good idea."

"Absolutely right," Fantasia's little hands fluttered together in delighted clapping, "but you just wait and see. You'll be so involved with all we show you, your task will seem a complete doddle. A walk in the park, as they say."

. . .

ALISON REMEMBERED Fantasia's words as she washed off the dust of the day that evening, using the shower sparingly. Appreciation of the value of water completely precluded soaking in the bath. She recollected image after image, small children outside huts; elders collected in the meagre shade of a lone thorn tree; boys herding their goats; women tending struggling crops. Although life was clearly experienced at a basic level, all the time there were smiles, waving hands and welcoming greetings. She'd been surprised to find so many small communities living in what seemed a vast empty expanse of bush and her heart had been warmed by the success of the Cleanwater projects she'd seen at work. Fantasia was a remarkable companion and she and her guide Walter and Lithulu the driver had made the day effortless and unforgettable. With a sigh of sheer enjoyment, Alison contemplated similar days ahead.

THE DAYS that followed were spent visiting Cleanwater projects and areas where new projects would begin, days in the Land Rover on dusty roads and off-roading through the bush. Alison sketched, made notes, used her camera and immersed herself in her surroundings, closely observing the people she met and absorbing their enthusiasm for the challenges they faced. Now Alison was finding it a pleasure to paint on the wide veranda at Golongwe, using sketches and photos collected over the last few days and appreciating the bright Southern Hemisphere light. People came and went from the Lodge; the liveried Land Rover deposited guests and staff went about their duties. Nobody seemed to notice Alison, tucked away in the cool shade at her easel. Deep in thought at times, she felt calm and content, absorbed by what she was doing and happy with her own company. Fantasia appeared in the afternoons to pass judgement, offer advice, gossip and drink gin when the sun went down. At last the task was almost complete and Alison was confident she had enough material to fulfil Felix's brief.

In the stillness of afternoon, heat pulsating silently at the edge of the veranda's shade, Fantasia leafed through paintings and sketches, discussing, sorting, asking, deliberating. Alison watched and listened and felt content to hear the criticism of this new friend whose opinion she instinctively respected. Fantasia's throaty voice, her jangling bangles and the rustle of paper being handled nibbled relentlessly at the hush surrounding them. At last she stood back and surveyed the assorted groups of paper.

"These pictures are so positive, Alison, so fresh; an ingénue looking at life. It amazes me that you haven't been painting all your life. I guess you had responsibilities which took up all your time and energy. But this world is new to you and I can see these scenes are observed by someone who's never seen them before. Look at this one." She held up a rough draft, pencil and watercolour, of a little boy sitting on an upturned rusty bucket with a hole in it beside a stagnant puddle. "The symbolism is all there. The water is the wrong sort of water and the bucket can't carry water anyway but the little boy is gazing up at you with a direct look and a wide smile. It tells the story. It's poignant yet charming. Your drawing is excellent and you've captured the harshness of the light with strong colours and I love the way you've achieved the shadows. You've clearly had good tuition."

Fantasia slipped her slight frame onto the lounger next to Alison's. The heat was lessening to a pleasant warmth and shadows of late afternoon deepened at the far edge of the lawn as Aidan invaded Alison's thoughts.

"Yes," she said softly, "really good tuition and the most lovely encouragement and support." She smiled at Fantasia.

"My tutor is a hugely tall person with a big personality who lives his life somewhat chaotically. You'd fit into his pocket, Fantasia."

Alison was surprised at Fantasia's seriousness as she regarded her in silence, drawing up her knees and putting her arms about them before she replied. "You love him, this tutor of yours?"

"I haven't really thought about it." Alison got up and carefully began to put her paintings and sketches together, handling them as though they might break, meticulously slipping them into protective cases. "And anyway, I'm not interested in loving anyone but the family I already have. I'm beginning to see myself as a different person. It's almost as though I can see my true identity. Is that ridiculous, at my age? But somehow I've shed the habit of years of being what everyone else expected me to be and now I can just be me." She laughed. "I sound like a self-help guru! But that *is* how I feel." She zipped the cases up vigorously and piled them neatly on the table.

Fantasia looked steadily up at her, chin still resting on her knees. "Hmmm," she murmured. "Sun's gone down. I'll ring for the gin."

NIGHT INSECTS JANGLED in the bush and stars spangled the velvet darkness as Fantasia put an ice-cold glass beside Alison.

"Don't you love this time of day?" Alison sighed deeply. "It was always the best time for me, the time between day and night. Transition. A change of clothes, a change of activity." She heard ice clink and felt cool condensation on her glass.

"What sort of activity?" asked Fantasia.

"Whatever James needed...I mean, whatever was in the diary for that night."

"James?" asked Fantasia.

"My former husband."

"Aaah. Hence the no more loving." Fantasia picked up her glass from the tray. Alison felt the warm night, the sound of the insects, the familiarity of this sudden nightfall wrap itself comfortingly about her. Fantasia brushed past her, giving her shoulder a little pat as she did so.

"I have no idea what went wrong," Alison said suddenly. "James retired. We came back to the UK and less than a week later he left me. For bloody Elspeth, career diplomat, just like him, but more than twenty years younger." She sipped her gin.

"So what do you feel now?" asked Fantasia.

"Well, I despise him really. He couldn't face up to retirement, ageing, not being Mr Big any more, not being important. So he hooked up with Elspeth and I imagine gets some vicarious satisfaction from being close to her career and reliving his own."

"I hope you don't mind if this sounds a little personal," Fantasia's voice was gentle, "But I've grown really fond of you over these last few days and I sense you're carrying a big burden. Perhaps I could help you to shed that burden?"

Alison's laugh was derisory. "Ha!" she barked, "All these months I've been struggling to understand why. Why, when I did so much to help James, to support him, to live my life to suit his requirements, uproot our children, be polite to people I hadn't the least interest in, live in great big unhomely houses, all for him! How is it you can do so much for the person you love and they can just walk out on you? I haven't got a burden, Fantasia. James is out of my life and I can do what I want. And I will never let anyone hurt me like that again."

"So there's no possibility of loving anyone else and this tutor of yours has no interest for you."

"I didn't say that," Alison was cautious. "But I suppose I might be afraid...afraid of trusting again. Afraid of getting it wrong again, of being hurt again."

"Here's a thought," said Fantasia. "You were so wonderfully capable and giving for all those years, did you ever ask James for help?"

"Well no, not really. I didn't need his help and anyway, he had important stuff to do and I got on with what was my role."

"Maybe you were too giving and too competent. Maybe part of Elspeth's attraction was needing his help? It's not necessarily a bad thing to be vulnerable, my friend. Creativity often comes from vulnerability and your creativity seems to me to be blossoming." Fantasia smiled gently at her and raised her glass encouragingly.

Alison exploded. "Vulnerable! Oh, I can be vulnerable. Put me anywhere near David Rowbottom and I say the wrong thing, or forget entirely what I was going to say, get in the way of his vehicle, even fall over! Twice!"

"David is your art tutor?"

"Oh. No, actually, the art tutor is called Aidan. David is someone else," Alison mumbled.

Fantasia laughed.

"Anyway, this conversation is academic," said Alison. "I am not in love. I am not going to be in love. I am not thinking about love. I can just be me."

"Love doesn't need thinking about!" exploded Fantasia. For a moment the insects were silent. "Love just is! You simply know it with every part of you, every fibre of your being; your singing heart and your soaring soul and your wide flung arms ready to embrace your love and the whole of the joyful world. What is there to think about? Don't think. Just love!"

Alison blinked in amazement. Where had all that come from? One minute a painting tutor and now a Grande Dame. Fantasia stood up, hands on hips. Clearly she hadn't finished yet.

"You," she wagged her finger at Alison, "are a painter. You are creative. You care about people, about the world. You are passionate but you put a lid on all this. You are so correct, so polite, so charming. You say you don't think about love. There is no need to think. Open your eyes and live. Remove the lid and be yourself. Just love. Don't think. Yes, you can be hurt. But you will mend. You can't love without risk. Take the risk! Believe me, I know what I'm saying. Remember, I have the wisdom of a very long life and I have loved for many years! How many years I will not tell you. Neither," she smiled, "will I tell you how many men I have loved."

26

O n the last painting day, Fantasia's words washed in and out of Alison's consciousness. Africa stretched away from her as far as she could see; dry land and sky with big flat-bottomed clouds moving north. I'll soon be following them, she thought; heading north to the cold and damp. Don't think. Just do. She banished thought. With her brush she mixed the golds and ochres and russets of the sunlit soil she saw about her and watched as women farmers began their work. The women bent and began to hoe rows into the earth. As she painted, Alison heard the rhythmic clink of the hoes as they moved along the stony rows. The soil was dry; the women were strong and their spirit was strong as they persevered with their work.

After hoeing came the planting, the small plants fragile, looking very alone in their rows, each one a distance from the other. Into the arid ochres and russets on her page Alison lightly introduced a pale, fragile green. Mealie plants. A vital staple food. She sat back and looked critically at her picture, at the dusty, sandy soil, the bright cloth of the bent women, the hoed rows and the fragile mealie plants. Now for the lifeline, the irrigation pipe, the product of efforts by Cleanwater. The scene needed the structure of the pipe, too, she thought. She took off her hat and fanned herself. A shadow passed over her picture.

"They said I'd find you here." Her hand stopped fanning. She was motionless. Was she breathing? "Hi there." David stood in front of her, blocking out the sun. She felt her jaw drop and quickly rectified the situation, clamping her mouth shut. Her heart raced as she opened her mouth again to speak.

"Good God. What are you doing here?"

David lowered himself onto a rock and Alison crammed her hat back onto her head. "Well, I thought I'd see how the painting was coming along."

She said nothing.

"How's it going?" He pushed his sunglasses upwards and leaned forward, frowning, looking intently at the picture. Alison watched him. He looked well. The tension was gone from his face. He was tanned and relaxed in his light polo shirt. His strong hands loosely clasped a stick between his knees. Still she said nothing. She sighed and smiled. It was undeniably good to see him. He looked at her, smiling back. There was stillness between them, a stillness in which Alison found herself acutely aware of David's nearness, his powerful frame, everything that was familiar about him. She sensed his vulnerability and his gentleness. As the stillness deepened she became uncomfortably aware of herself, creased and crumpled, dusty and dishevelled. She lifted a hand to push her hair off her face and David reached out and took it, held it firmly, raised an eyebrow, challenging her to withdraw it. She didn't. He lifted her hand and brushed her folded fingers gently with his lips.

"Do you recall our conversation," he said, "at the Cleanwater event?"

Alison shook her head.

"You don't?" David returned her hand to her. "I said one

of the most important things of my life and you don't remember it?"

Again she shook her head.

"I don't remember a conversation," said Alison as the evening in the Village Hall reassembled itself in rural Africa. "I remember you arriving late and doing your own thing and that was that."

"Don't you remember anything at all I said to you?" His eyes were wide with astonishment.

She shrugged. "I had a lot of responsibility that evening and as long as we got the exhibition opened that was all that mattered to me. And open it you did. I regret I wasn't a Hal Davidson groupie that evening, and that I didn't hang on to every word you uttered." She looked at him innocently.

"And to think I thought of you as Little Red Riding Hood. Could it be you're the wolf in grandmother's clothing? You certainly know how to crush a person." Did she see the light in his eye dim a little? Was there unfamiliar hesitancy in his relaxed demeanour? Surely not. He was smiling. "I am not an intuitive person. I'm not sensitive and artistic like you. But I have come a very long way to tell you something, so I'm going to tell you and then I'll get into my jeep over there and go all the way back...if you'd like me to." He shifted on his rock and his fingers twisted round his stick.

She couldn't resist it. She had to speak. "So you would like me to be a Hal Davidson groupie, would you; to sit here and drink in your every word?"

"You really are the most infuriating woman. Alison, that night in the Village Hall I said you had brought the colour back into my life. And I meant it. When I got back from my tour you were gone! Without a word! Highvale was empty. England was empty. My life was empty. I didn't like it. I couldn't write. The sun didn't shine. Nothing mattered. It was appalling. I had to find you, had to come to Africa and here I am. I have to have you in my life."

His arrogance took her breath away. "Nothing changes, does it," she said. "You don't change. Ever since I first saw you, all you thought of was yourself, and that's exactly what you're doing now. As long as you have what you want, you'll blaze your own trail across anyone else's life without a thought for them." But her anger was solely intellectual. She knew her heart was singing and her soul was soaring. David laughed. He laughed! How dare he? She was furious! Awkwardly he stood and held out his hand.

"Come here," he said, "come close to me and I promise you, you won't regret it. Come and fly with me. You and I have both known pain. We know what it feels like to have the life you thought was yours taken away from you and we know how to face a challenge. You and I. Now is not the time to play safe. Now is the time to fly. You know it and I know it. I can see you feel it too. Come on Madam, what do you say? Come and fly with me." She took his hand, laughing, Fantasia's words of passion chiming in her head.

"You are my love," he said. "You are the first and the last. I knew it the moment I saw you teetering about the country lanes in your shiny boots and your pale winter coat. Now there's a girl who'll take risks, I thought. And then you offered me your magnificent sarcasm and my heart was captured." Alison heard the sound of clapping hands as David bent to kiss her. As he wrapped his arms about her she felt the warmth of the African sun and the approval of the ladies with their hoes and then nothing mattered but David.

THE UNWARMED SKY was still steel grey as a light aircraft landed and taxied on the bumpy airstrip. Standing on the steps of the small terminal building, Alison smiled at David and reflected on her deep and surprising contentment. It was as if her life had been an unfinished jigsaw and now the last piece had fallen into place.

"You have been a great surprise to me," she said. "I was quite determined I would never again be in a position where I loved someone so much that they could hurt me."

She saw pain cloud his face and he was swiftly by her side, his arm around her.

"I can't bear to think of you in pain," he said, his voice soft and gentle; his lips brushing the nape of her neck. "Whatever hurt there is to be I'll share with you, I'll lift from you, I'll ease for you. But it will never be me who hurts you." She saw the conviction in his eyes and felt the confident strength of his arm around her and believed him. She was happy.

"So would you say we're about to blaze a trail northwards?" She smiled up at him.

"I certainly would. And what a trail it's going to be." He winced as he repositioned his leg and shifted his weight, leaning on his stick. "The guys will put the bags on board for us. We just have to wait for the disembarking passengers."

With a sense of deep contentment and wholeness, standing comfortably close to David, Alison watched a small group of people make their way towards the steps where she stood. Then she tensed, stood up straight, shaded her eyes against the rising sun.

"Alison? What is it?" David sensed her tension. Leading the troop of passengers was a tall, thin and impeccably groomed young woman, head held high, purposeful stride ensuring she was ahead of the rest. As they reached the bottom of the steps she turned to face the man who was following her, a stooping grey-haired man in a safari suit, laden with assorted bags.

"Do come along James," she called. "I'd rather not keep my official welcoming party waiting," and she strode up the steps and into the building.

"James," Alison whispered. The man had adjusted the lilac silk jacket he was carrying and rearranged his camera bag, laptop bag, cabin bag and a large quilted pink holdall and negotiated the steps. At the top he looked up and saw Alison. He dropped the jacket and the holdall.

"Good God," he said, "Ali."

Alison smiled. "James," she said.

"You look...you look," he stuttered, "...you look wonderful." He scratched his head and blinked behind heavy-rimmed glasses.

Alison's spirit soared. She turned to David. "David," she said formally, "May I introduce you to James Henderson?" With a graceful gesture she indicated the bright jacket and pink holdall resting on the dusty floor. "Hadn't you better rescue your belongings? Do forgive us," she smiled radiantly, "But there's no time to catch up. We have a trail to blaze."

Alison walked to the plane blissfully happy. She knew she'd live the day in the moment, no past, no future, only the present, with arms outstretched to embrace the world, to embrace life. It was a good way to live, she thought.

ABOUT THE AUTHOR

For twenty years, Fiona Fieldhouse was an expatriate in Africa, India, the Far East and Europe. Her professional expertise is management of end-of-life nursing care. She has travelled from the brittleness of the Embassy cocktail party to the bedside of human frailty and the richness of life at both these extremes fuels her compulsion to write.

INTERVIEW WITH THE AUTHOR

What inspired you to write this book?

I have always loved the idea of romance between the unlikeliest people. Life and circumstance throw two people together and they mistakenly think they're experiencing true dislike, but in fact it's an instant attraction.

I woke up one morning with this book in my head. Where it came from, I have no idea. There was David, in his wheel-chair, hugely frustrated by his immobility and dependency and along came fragile, uncertain Alison. For each of them, at this moment in their lives, the last thing either of them want is the vulnerability of falling in love. So what happens? This novel happened.

I have been writing all my life; stories as a teenager, letters home when living abroad, professional reports when working, and eventually when my children were grown up I had the time and opportunity to undertake creative writing courses and learn the craft of this magical creative enterprise. To me it is indeed magic, that I can read words on a page, words written by a person I will never meet in a time and place far from my own, and be transported into another world. So when David and Alison popped into my head, off I went.

It is said that a writer's own biography can appear in fiction. In truth, I was a trailing spouse for many years, a role you see far less these days, and for us it really was a case of 'follow your man', and you were identified with your husband's occupation. I will never forget being greeted at a party in Africa with the words, 'Oh hello, you must be Mrs British Airways. I'm Mrs Standard Bank.' So this experience was close to my heart and guiding Alison through her new beginning and her rediscovery of herself was, for me, compelling. I could not say no.

What has *Alison's New Beginnings* taught you about writing?

I have learned what a mammoth task it is to get 70,000 words onto the page; the time it takes, the persistence required, the denial of many other things one should be doing in order to fulfil the compulsion to tell the story. I have learned to trust the characters in my care, to let them respond and react in their own way. And I have learned that the most important person of all is the reader, for whom this whole creative enterprise happens.

What are you writing next ?

I have a novel awaiting a rewrite, a memoir almost completed and several short stories needing organisation into a collection. So I have much to do for my reader. The wonderful thing about being, shall we say, of mature years, is that you have a bag full of stuff to write about and now is the time to tip it all out and share it.

If you enjoyed this book, please help to spread the word by leaving a review on Amazon, Goodreads, Kobo or any other suitable site. These are of immense value to new authors. On social media, you can join the conversation using the hashtag #Alisonsnewbeginnings where Fiona loves to see photos of the book in all the different locations her readers are found. If you'd like to keep in touch with Fiona Fieldhouse and her writings, or send feedback, please email her publisher on contact@offthepressbooks.com

Saving Francesca Maier

Claire Wingfield

'Just gorgeous. Captures fraught relationships with subtlety and wisdom.' Julia Gray

'Moving and beautifully written…explores the complex ties of family and friendship with insight and compassion.' Tracey Emerson

Can you leave the past in another country?

Francesca Maier knows little of her father's home country or her parents' life together before she was born. A summer in Berlin brings the past – and its secrets – alive. Adrift in a foreign city, she finds an unexpected friend in east Berliner Antonio – but what will he sacrifice to save her?

Saving Francesca Maier probes the secrets every family hides and the choices we make in a volatile world.

Contains writing prompts and author interview, making this the perfect Book Club read

£8.99

ISBN 978-0957527928

ACKNOWLEDGMENTS

I would like to thank the kind and generous people whose early reading and valuable honesty guided me. They know who they are. And also Claire Wingfield at Off The Press Books for her professional expertise and her unwavering belief in *Alison's New Beginnings*.